Dastardly Deeds
in
Victorian Warwickshire

Dastardly Deeds

in

Victorian Warwickshire

Graham Sutherland

BREWIN
BOOKS

First Published by Brewin Books Ltd
Studley, Warwickshire. B80 7LG
in June 1999

British Library Cataloguing In Publication Data.
A Catalogue record for this book is available
from The British Library

ISBN 1 85858 143 5

Typeset in Baskerville.
Made and printed in Great Britain by
SupaPrint (Redditch) Ltd

ACKNOWLEDGEMENTS

The author gratefully acknowledges all the help given to him by Solihull Metropolitan Borough Council Education, Libraries and Arts Department: Warwickshire County Record Office: Warwickshire Constabulary History Society: Claire for the long term loan of her Encyclopaedia of Illustration: and lastly Trish who had the unenviable task of typing the original manuscript. A big thank you to you all.

CONTENTS

ILLUSTRATIONS

The Greenways in Court at Warwick 1887.
(Picture - Courtesy of Warwickshire County Record Office)

1

I DID MY DUTY

(1842 – Spernall)

On a December day in 1844 James Crowley sat enjoying a quiet drink at the *Castle & Falcon* in Chester. Relaxed and probably thinking about his next meeting with Miss Garner, it is doubtful if he noticed the two men coming towards him.

Suddenly they pounced and James was hurled to the floor. In a moment his assailants handcuffed him and announced they were police officers. Thus Warwickshire's most wanted man was arrested.

The story really began some three years earlier. Crowley's father William farmed at Spernall near Alcester. To say he did not get on with his son is an understatement. They had a very stormy relationship which worsened when James published a pamphlet complaining of his father's tyrannical attitude towards him. It fuelled the rumours about insanity in the family.

During the coming year their relationship deteriorated further. By Christmas 1842 William was so frightened of James he had several of his employees sworn in as Special Constables.

They have the same powers as their counterparts, take the same risks and occasionally suffer the consequences. Unlike their 19th century ancestors, today's Specials are all volunteers. Traditionally the Special Constabulary could, and did, call upon men to join their ranks as necessary in times of emergency. Harsh penalties were available for anyone who refused. Understandably most men joined the ranks when required. Farm labourer William Tilsley was one and he took his duties seriously.

Christmas Day 1842 on the Crowley farm would be remembered for many years. About mid-morning James was seen walking across the fields towards his father's house. On the way he saw one of William's labourers and called out cryptically, "I will lay them asleep before I sleep tonight", after which he vanished. He reappeared later wearing his best clothes and carrying a double barrelled gun.

The constables saw him go round the outside of the farmhouse towards the dining room where he knew his father would be. As they moved to follow him there came the sound of smashing glass. Breaking into a run, Tilsley led the way round the house out of sight of his comrades.

Following his lead they heard him call out to James, but the only reply was the sound of a shot. Slowing down they moved cautiously round the corner. Tilsley was lying in a pool of blood. Having been shot through the eye, he had died instantaneously. In the ensuing confusion James escaped. Soon afterwards one of the constables found him saddling a horse. Petrified he stood rooted to the ground as the fugitive turned towards him. James looked at him coldly as he mounted his horse. "I've done for me" was all he said, and moments later rode away. He left behind a very relieved constable.

By the time John Findon, the Alcester constable arrived, James had long since fled. In spite of a lengthy search no trace was found of him. Later it was reported he had fled to America. There the matter rested until 13 December 1844 when James was arrested in Chester.

He was taken to Warwick Gaol. When charged with Tilsley's murder, he replied, "I did my duty." It was another of his cryptic messages which nobody fully understood. In early April 1845 James stood trial at Warwick Assizes.

His trial was sensational. Being the first murder case to be heard in the County for some years, it quickly became a great social occasion. Admission to the actual hearing was by ticket only. The court room rapidly filled to suffocation point with the local press reporting several respectable families amongst the spectators.

Although James pleaded "not guilty" he could not really contest the prosecution evidence. His Counsel had a difficult fight on his hands.

Needless to say he concentrated on the 'insanity' of his client including the rumours about the family in the absence of William Crowley, who had since died. He outlined how James had gone to America and returned to England still using the name of Crowley. "Was this the action of a sane man?" he argued. Another eleven witnesses followed, each testifying to there being 'something strange' about James.

Next he claimed James had no real wish to harm his father and the gun had gone off accidentally, although he omitted to give any valid reason for it being loaded in the first place. Further allegations followed quickly about the prosecution fabricating their evidence.

Relentlessly he continued attacking the prosecution by accusing the arresting officers of 'having acted gleefully' in expectation of receiving a reward. Of course he forgot, conveniently, to inform the court how James was armed with a loaded double barrelled pistol when arrested. He argued how the lapse of time between the offence and the trial was a good reason for James to be acquitted!

In fact he almost succeeded. After being out for nearly two hours, the Jury returned and found James guilty, adding they did so reluctantly. Their view was not shared by the judge who quickly sentenced James to death.

In the following days a petition was raised begging for mercy for James. Other similar letters were published, including one by the Under Sheriff of the County. No thought was given to William Tilsley who had been murdered whilst performing his duty. By now James had become the victim.

At 10 o'clock on Friday 18 April 1845 James knew his pleas for mercy had not been heeded. With St Mary's church bells tolling mournfully in the background, the 31 year old drank wine before stepping out onto the scaffold. With a steady gaze he looked at the assembled crowed and was duly hanged.

William Tilsley figures but little in this sorry tale, but he became the first police officer to be murdered in Warwickshire. As for James, undoubtedly he was insane and as such, should he have been hanged?

QUEENS EVIDENCE

(1844 – Radway)

"Who's there?" called Mary Chambers in a frightened voice as she looked at the moving light under her bedroom door. She knew it might be her maid, but, somehow doubted it was. She did not have long to wait for her worst fears to be realised.

Suddenly the door was thrust open and three men rushed into her bedroom. Their leader immediately pointed a pistol at her forehead and demanded money and the keys to her bureau. By the candle he held in his other hand, Mary could see all three men had blackened faces. She was aware of a fourth person out in the passageway, no doubt waiting to deal with her maid if necessary. Absolutely terrified Mary quickly handed over her keys to the men.

John Bratt from Neithrop was the evil genius behind the raid. He knew how elderly Mary was an invalid and confined to a downstairs room, with only her maid, Sally, to keep her company. But she was reputed to be very wealthy and would not be expected to offer much, if any, resistance.

Bratt seemed to lead a charmed life. He had been acquitted in court over the years of various charges including murder. He had a reputation to live up to and was not short of followers. For this raid he had Thomas Perry recruit his accomplices and make enquiries about Mary Chambers. The other two members of the gang were Sidney Conway and Frederick Grey. By letting Perry do the recruiting and research, Bratt could remain in the background making it easier for him to deny being involved if anything went wrong.

On the evening of 16 December 1844 Conway went to bed in his parent's house at Bascote as usual. To avoid arousing their suspicions he climbed out of the window and met up with Perry and Grey. Together they walked to Radway and where Bratt was waiting for them. He wore a fustian jacket with white buttons underneath a blue apron. Conway lent him a pistol he had obtained and all four blackened their faces. Making their way to the Manor House they broke open the cellar door and entered. Soon they had forced their way into Mary's bedroom.

After menacing Mary with the pistol Bratt threatened to kill her maid if she tried to enter the bedroom. Mary was forced to watch them ransack her bureau where she kept her money. Afterwards she heard them moving about elsewhere in the house before all went quiet. It is not difficult to imagine her relief when daylight came and the men left her house.

For the next few days Mary was still too terrified to tell anybody about what had happened. Nobody would have been any the wiser if it had not been for John Washbrook, a farm labourer. On going up to the house he saw the forced open cellar door and realised quickly what had happened. He wasted no time in summoning John Coles the local constable

Coles instigated a thorough search of the house. Three musical boxes, £10, and various items of silver plate including spoons were found to have been stolen. After gently coaxing Mary he obtained descriptions of the missing property and the raiders, which he circulated around the area, including nearby Banbury. Somebody offered £100 reward and all Coles could do was to sit back and wait.

Meanwhile the raiders had shared out the spoils and gone about their normal business. Conway hid his share among the thatch and grounds of his parent's house. Grey, however, was too impatient and decided to sell the spoons. He had his sister, Eliza, take them into Banbury. It was to prove a grave error.

Coles's circulation had paid dividends and the spoons were recognised. Whilst the intended purchaser kept Eliza talking, one of his assistants went for the police. Daniel Newton, the Neithrop constable was on the scene quickly and Eliza was detained. It did not take long to discover the name and address of her brother. Soon

Grey, Perry and Conway had been arrested and most of Mary's property recovered. However, there was not sign of Bratt.

After his initial appearance in Court, Conway asked to see the magistrates. He confessed his part in the burglary and told them where he had hidden his share of the proceeds. Later he offered to turn Queen's Evidence against his partners in crime for a suitable reward. His offer was accepted. Meanwhile Bratt had been traced to a brothel in Warwick.

Quietly the Warwick Constables assembled their posse before going after him. Only when the premises were surrounded did one of them knock on the door and demand admittance. Hearing the commotion Bratt realised they had come for him. His first intention was to escape through a window, but a quick look outside told him he stood no chance. He was not too unduly worried as he had a hiding place arranged inside the house. It was an old cupboard something like a priest's hole. It had the advantage of being very difficult to see unless someone was actually in the room. But Constable John Neale was not easily fooled. He had become suspicious about the size of the room which did not seem to tally with the outside measurements. Then he found the cupboard, and on opening it found Bratt whom he promptly arrested.

For various reasons the trial at Warwick Assizes did not take place until the following August. Only Bratt, Grey and Perry were charged and they pleaded not guilty. Conway kept his part of the deal and became a witness for the prosecution. His evidence was fairly damning. The jury took about twenty minutes to reach a verdict of guilty against all three defendants. The mills of justice grind slowly but at last they had caught up with Bratt when he and the other two men were each sentenced to fifteen years transportation. Conway was freed.

3

THE LEIGH INHERITANCE

(1848 – Stoneleigh)

Charles Griffin felt a glow of satisfaction. At last he had fulfilled his ambition: his book was written. Now he could set the record straight and prove Lord Chandos Leigh was not the rightful owner of the Stoneleigh Abbey Estate.

Entitled "Stoneleigh Abbey – Thirty Four Years Ago" Griffin's book read like a typical melodramatic Victorian novel. Centred around a disputed inheritance it ended with a programme of mass murder to protect the current owners of the estate. Whilst the book may have read like a novel, in reality it was an undisguised attack on Lord Leigh and his family. They did not find the book at all entertaining and Lord Leigh's patience with Griffin was beginning to wear out.

The tale really began in 1786 when an article appeared in the Gentlemen's Magazine concerning the succession of the Leigh family to the Stoneleigh Abbey Estate. The actual article was relatively unimportant until a copy of it came into the possession of a certain George Leigh. He considered his family had a far better claim to the estate and set about trying to put the record straight. The magazine article was used to support his unsuccessful claim.

In 1806 Mary Leigh died and the estate passed ultimately to Chandos Leigh who was to experience a great deal of problems concerning his inheritance. By 1843 the efforts of several other claimants had been disposed of successfully by Chandos. Believing his problems to now be over, Chandos settled down to enjoy some peace. Little did he realise his troubles were far from over and the next few years were to be quite eventful.

During the evening of Friday 18 October 1844 a small group of men was seen approaching the Abbey. As it happened Lord Leigh and his family were away and solicitor George Jones had been left in charge. Hearing of the men's approach, George ordered the gates to be closed before they arrived. On reaching the Abbey they demanded the gates be opened which George refused. They departed after a few minutes leaving George with an unhappy feeling he had not seen the last of them and they would be back.

His fears were confirmed on Monday morning when a considerably larger group returned. George was alarmed to see how many of them were armed with sticks and cudgels. However, he had been busy during the weekend and the servants had been reinforced by Police Sergeant Elijah Dencer and other officers. They had taken up temporary residence in the Abbey. Initially George attempted to reason with the mob but quickly realised he was wasting his time.

James Leigh, who was one of the ringleaders, challenged George's right to be at the Abbey. Ignoring George's reply he began kicking down the housekeeper's door. It was the signal for the beginning of a general assault on the Abbey. Sergeant Dencer tried to disarm James Leigh but was hit over the head for his pains. The mob streamed past George and the remaining heavily outnumbered police officers and had little difficulty in taking over the Abbey. It was thought, at one stage, they were looking for firearms. In the confusion George escaped and went to Leamington for help.

Later that day a posse of six police officers, supported by twenty two Special Constables, under the command of Superintendent William Roby, of the Leamington Borough Police, marched on the Abbey. They were accompanied by George and followed by numerous spectators who eagerly anticipated an entertaining afternoon. Although the Abbey had been well barricaded in George's absence, the invaders surrendered without a struggle. John Leigh, one of the claimants was the last to surrender. He did so by formally handing the keys of the Abbey back to George.

The prisoners were taken back to Leamington Town Hall where a special court had been arranged. In a crowded courtroom they were each charged with offences of riot, breaking into Stoneleigh Abbey in addition to assaulting servants and constables. James Leigh elected to conduct the defence on behalf of the prisoners and did so in a very spirited manner. He scored several points over the prosecution, in particular with their use of George Jones. James objected to him being both witness and prosecutor. The magistrates, one of whom was the renowned Dr Henry Jephson, agreed. George was instructed to direct his questions through them.

James admitted there had been some violence used when taking over the Abbey. However, he blamed the police for starting it! On another occasion he disagreed so vehemently the magistrates ordered him to be quiet. Bitterly he retorted how he had been quiet enough for the past 30 years since his family had been robbed of the estate! At the end of the hearing two women and a man were acquitted, but the remainder were committed for trial as the next Assizes. In the meantime there was growing concern about the condition of two of the servants who had been injured in the attack. Luckily they made a full recovery.

The following month the case was tried at Warwick Assizes. The hearing was divided into two parts. One involved just the ringleaders and the other involved the followers. By now the initial charges had been reduced and only the assault allegations were tried. All the defendants were found guilty. Bearing in mind all the facts of the case, the judge was quite lenient with the followers. They each received a three month prison sentence but without hard labour.

As expected, the ringleaders were not so lucky. With the exception of James Leigh, they each received a twelve month sentence in the house of correction. James was clearly the overall leader of the group. He had not hesitated to use violence to further his own aims, regardless of whether lives were lost or not. Consequently the judge decided to make an example of him. His sentence was eighteen months imprisonment. All the ringleaders would carry out hard labour whilst in prison.

As there had been some public sympathy towards the prisoners, Lord Leigh found himself on the receiving end of outbursts of abuse from various people until matters slowly returned to normal. He had been so pleased with the courage shown by his housekeeper, Jane Savoury, during the attack, that he gave her a massive teapot as a reminder of the event. She was most impressed.

Also impressed by the affair, but for a very different reason, was solicitor Charles Griffin. He was well known for his anti aristocracy views being reputed to be involved with Chartism. As part of the defence team he had been intrigued by James Leigh and his gang. Whilst working on their case Griffin had uncovered some interesting information about the Leigh family past and present and became totally obsessed by the mystery of the Leigh inheritance. Painstakingly he began gathering evidence against them and waited for a suitable moment to strike.

In the meantime Griffin continued researching and amassing a considerable amount of knowledge about the Leigh family. He even toured the country lecturing on the subject. In early 1848 the collapse of Chartism gave him more time to devote to the subject. On 13 May 1848 everything was ready and he made his move.

At the County Petty Sessions Griffin made an application for a warrant to search the Stoneleigh Abbey Estate for the bodies of at least four itinerant workers. These were men who had not been seen, allegedly, since 1814 when the new bridge was built across the river at Stoneleigh. Griffin explained how up to 30 men had been systematically murdered by the then Lord Leigh, his family and members of the estate staff. Their bodies had been buried in different parts of the estate and Griffin wanted to find some of them.

According to Griffin, the victims had been participants in a plot by the then Lord Leigh to remove all traces of other members of the family, who might threaten his line of succession. His allegations came as no surprise to those who knew of his interests. He alleged certain monuments had been removed from Stoneleigh Church, not that it could now be proved they ever existed. Tales of the removal of name plates from coffins in the family vault had been heard before. It was after the disappearance of these items, argued Griffin, that the mass murders began of the itinerant workers who had helped in their removal.

It was an amazing narrative which stirred the imagination of those who heard if for the first time. A few workmen, alleged Griffin, had been shot by the gamekeeper, some had been clubbed to death with hammers. The most fanciful tale revealed how masonry from the new bridge had been dropped onto others.

Lord Leigh was adamant he had nothing to hide, but refused permission for the bridge to be excavated as Griffin wanted. Apart from costing £10,000 he emphasised the search would reveal nothing. He pleaded with the magistrates and emphasised no bodies were to be found on the estate. They agreed with him and dismissed Griffin's application.

It would have been very much in Griffin's interest to have let the matter rest at this stage, but he was not prepared to do so and persisted in his campaign against the Leigh family. Three months later he charged Chandos Leigh with murder.

Once again he tried, unsuccessfully to obtain search warrants, particularly for the bridge abutments. In support of his allegations he produced Richard Barnett, an itinerant workman, who had worked on the bridge. Barnett spoke about two of his fellow workmen who had worked on the bridge. They had vanished about ten minutes before mortar was put on the abutments. Immediately after the last stone had been bedded in, he testified to seeing blood seep around the edges. He went on to tell the magistrates about the bodies he had seen in the coal-house sewn up in sacks. Later these too were buried in the bridge foundations at the dead of night.

Under cross-examination Barnett admitted having run away from Stoneleigh to save his life. He remained a plausible witness until identified as a convicted criminal. Faced with little alternative Barnett agreed, but claimed he had been wrongly convicted and was totally innocent. His answers became more fanciful. Then he accused the Leigh family of personally dropping the stone into the abutment where the bodies had been placed. When it was established how Barnett had been in contact with some of the claimants to the estate, his evidence lost all credibility. Worse followed. As he left the witness box the magistrates had him arrested and committed to gaol for perjury!

With Barnett's evidence totally discredited, Griffin cannot have been surprised when the magistrates dismissed the charge against Lord Leigh. Whatever course of action Griffin may have planned next never took place as Lord leigh took the offensive. Suddenly Griffin found himself being sued for libel.

The case went before Warwick Assizes in early 1849. It was another spectacular event and lasted for five days in a crowded courtroom. Right from its outset Griffin was in serious trouble. Barnett's evidence might have helped , but his star witness had disappeared. Clearly Barnett had decided not to be involved any further: undoubtedly a wise decision. Griffin's last hope was to be allowed to use Barnett's deposition in evidence. However, this was not to be as the judge would not allow it to be used. The long suffering Lord Leigh was treated sympathetically with little or none going to the defendant. Griffin was found guilty.

In the expectant hush which followed, Griffin was sentenced to two years in prison with hard labour. In addition he would have to provide £500 in his own surety with further sureties each in the sum of £250 to be of good behaviour for two years following his release. Griffin protested about not having access to such money. The judge replied he should have thought about the possible consequences before embarking on his campaign against Lord Leigh.

4

THE CHARLECOTE BURGLARY

(1850 – Charlecote)

O n entering the library at Charlecote House, butler John Forster stopped. Something was very wrong. A window and several cabinets had been forced open. A quick check showed various items to the value of £400 were missing. They included a miniature painting of Sir Thomas Lucy. The house had been burgled.

It was 7 May 1850 and Charlecote, like many parts of Warwickshire, did not enjoy the luxury of a proper police force. The residents were obliged to rely on the efforts of the local parish constable to uphold the law for them. In this instance he did his best and within a few hours the details of the stolen property had been widely circulated. Two days later they came to the notice of Inspector George Glossop of the Birmingham City Detective Force. He waited long enough to collect Constable William Dutton before hurrying off to where John Evans and John Bradshaw rented rooms.

Although five years younger, Bradshaw was the leader of the two. He was a prolific criminal, wanted by the police and an escapee from Worcester Gaol. Undoubtedly it was his idea to burgle Charlecote House but Evans needed little encouragement. On 6 May 1850 they had travelled separately to Warwick. For the next few hours they left a whole trail of clues behind them which a child could have followed.

Meeting up in the *Crown Hotel* they played the part of tourists, visiting the Castle and other interesting sites. Bradshaw kept a meticulous record in his pocket book of the places visited and the money they spent. Later they met up again in the *Crown Hotel* before moving on to Barford, continually drawing attention to themselves.

Whether it was an act of bravado or stupidity was never established.

In Barford they went to the *George Inn* where they ordered tea, but left before it was served. On leaving Barford they met a young boy whom they questioned about the occupier of Charlecote House. He told them it was a Mrs Lucy and Bradshaw replied, "That's it", and walked away. The boy could not help noticing how both men carried carpet bags.

4 am saw them passing the time of day with a stonemason by Charlecote House. Later other witnesses saw them on the canal tow path before catching a bus to Birmingham where no doubt, they thought they would be safe. But George Glossop had other ideas.

On arriving at the men's rooms, Glossop discovered they were both out. Undeterred the police officers entered and prepared to wait. They used the time profitably and made a careful search. Among the items they found were a picklock, centre bit and dark lantern; all part of a burglar's trade. They were concerned to discover a pistol, bullets and powder flasks.

At about 7 pm Bradshaw returned and entered his room. Caught completely unawares the officers were able to arrest him before he had a chance to struggle. Once he was secured, Glossop opened the bag Bradshaw had been carrying. Inside he found the stolen miniature painting and a broken fruit knife. Also in the bag was a fully loaded double barrelled pistol which Bradshaw had been unable to use. Evans did not return and Glossop had to be content with Bradshaw.

Next day Glossop went to Charlecote House with the implements he had seized from Bradshaw. The painting was readily identified. After comparing the broken fruit knife with some marks at the windows and cabinets, he found they matched exactly. As an added bonus he found the other part of the broken knife.

On his return to Birmingham Glossop searched Bradshaw's room again and found the pocket book detailing their visit to Warwick. Only Evans remained free, but Glossop had the matter in hand. Believing Evans would contact his sister at some time, he arranged for her mail to be intercepted. Five days later his resourcefulness was rewarded when Evans wrote to his sister asking for money to be sent to an address in Liverpool. It did not take long for him to be arrested and brought back to Warwick Gaol.

As the evidence against the men was gathered numerous witnesses came forward who had seen them during the day. Once an identification had taken place in the gaol, the case was complete. On 6 August they appeared at Warwick Assizes where they pleaded not guilty to charges of burglary and receiving stolen property.

The evidence was straight forward until Glossop testified. For some inexplicable reason he became hesitant and evasive about certain issues, especially the finding of the fruit knife. He claimed he had forgotten about it until he was pressed. In spite of this, the jury found them guilty. They were both sentenced to transportation: Evans for ten years and Bradshaw for fifteen.

When he was arrested Bradshaw was in possession of £43.10s in cash. The jury decided unanimously that this money belonged to Mrs Lucy and should be given to her. The judge agreed but ordered £5 of it should be given to Glossop for his outstanding work on the case.

Whilst awaiting transportation Bradshaw heard about the numerous rumours circulating about Glossop. It was suggested he was not as honest as everyone thought. Bradshaw added to them when he wrote to the High Sheriff accusing Glossop of not effecting his arrest until the right reward was available. Finally he accused Glossop of knowing about the burglary before it happened and demanding his share of the proceeds. The rumours continued growing and Glossop was accused of being involved in other burglaries.

By now the authorities were beginning to doubt the policeman's integrity. They queried how he had known just where to find Evans and Bradshaw. And there was the matter of his forgetfulness in court. A full scale enquiry into Glossop's activities was commenced. Eventually he was cleared and the allegation declared to be 'false and unfounded'. Yet the rumours persisted especially among the county authorities. They ceased only after Glossop had threatened to sue the parties involved.

5

JUST REWARD

(1852 – Leamington)

Elizabeth Allen was suspicious of the two men in her husband's shop in Leamington Spa. There was something not quite right about them. Even after they had paid her 1d. for a piece of tape she remained on edge. Her eyes never left them as they moved towards the door. Suddenly, one of them grabbed some gloves and they both ran out into the night hotly pursued by Elizabeth.

She was delighted to find Police Constable William Hunt nearby and breathlessly told him what had happened. He set off in pursuit accompanied by witness Henry Duckett. Some minutes later William had both men in custody and the expectation of a reward.

Twenty-two years old, William had been a police officer for just six months. He was a keen and efficient officer with fourteen previous arrests to his credit. The arrest of John Dwyer and a man called Perks brought the total to sixteen: at the time of their arrest, 8 December 1852, it was the accepted practice in Leamington for magistrates to reward diligent police officers. The going rate for an arrest was £0 5s 0d.(25p). This was the equivalent of two days pay for policemen and was a considerable financial incentive to encourage diligence by officers. Such a practice is not without its dangers.

In due course Perks and Dwyer were sentenced to six months imprisonment for this and other petty crimes. William collected his reward and life continued as normal. Meanwhile in Warwick Gaol, Dwyer spent his time talking to and listening to the other prisoners. He learned some interesting facts and began to scheme. At the end of their sentence, Perks left the area whilst Dwyer went to Leamington.

He waited in a dark street until a police officer slowly approached. Dwyer maintained he had always intended to confront Hunt and believed this shadowy figure to be him. In fact it was Constable Samuel Hill whom he approached. Dwyer told him an interesting tale. Hill listened aghast, hardly able to believe what he had heard and not wanting to believe it. Seeking corroboration, he invited Constable William Moore to join them from a neighbouring beat. Dwyer repeated his story. Realising the gravity of Dwyer's allegation, they advised him to repeat his story to their Superintendent, William Roby.

Consequently, the following Sunday Dwyer went to see the Superintendent, but found his way blocked by William Hunt. The Officer asked outright what Dwyer was going to say to Roby. Dwyer did not hesitate in telling him everything, including the tales he had heard whilst in gaol. Hunt was thoroughly scared by what he heard. As a desperate measure he offered Dwyer 1s. 6d. (9p) to leave Leamington for good without seeing Roby. He agreed, took the money and left in the opposite direction. Much relieved, Hunt went about his duties believing that to be the end of the matter. He was sadly mistaken.

Unbeknown to him, Amelia Blencoe had seen the two men talking and she was one of Roby's servants. Next day Dwyer returned and saw Roby. The Superintendent listened with growing concern to Dwyer's narrative. It sounded far fetched and no doubt Roby was inclined to disbelieve it.

Dwyer's story was simple enough. He alleged it had been Hunt's idea to steal the gloves from Mrs Allen. In fact, he added, the Constable had even given them the money to purchase the tape. Finally, Dwyer alleged Hunt was the mastermind behind other thefts. It had just been bad luck Elizabeth Allen had seen Hunt when she did and he had been forced to arrest Dwyer and Perks. His story finished, Dwyer departed leaving Roby in a quandary not knowing what to believe. Then Amelia told him about seeing Hunt with Dwyer the previous day. It tended to make him believe there was some truth in the allegations.

As Roby began asking questions, the evidence against Hunt grew. Witnesses had seen the three men talking together just before the theft. Any lingering doubts he may have had were quickly dispelled when Hunt failed to report for duty and could not be found anywhere in Leamington. After much hard work he was traced to Yorkshire, having changed his name to Howard, where he was employed as a workman. Following a violent struggle he was arrested and returned to Leamington. From there it was a short journey to Warwick Gaol.

In April 1853 Hunt appeared at Warwick Assizes where he was charged with three counts of theft, mainly of clothing, from premises in Leamington. He pleaded not guilty to all charges.

His only defence relied on a total denial of the prosecution's allegations. Both Perks and another witness had left the area and could not corroborate Dwyer's accusations. Great play was made on Hunt's previous good character. Even Roby agreed he had been a good officer. The prosecution systematically attacked by concentrating on the flaws in Hunt's version.

Why had he absconded to Yorkshire? Changed his name to Howard? And resisted arrest? Other searching questions followed. In reply, Hunt stated he was frightened of being transported in the event of being found guilty. It was a feeble excuse. Fighting to the very last, the defence insisted Dwyer's allegations were all fabrications in an attempt to get revenge. Even Dwyer's meeting with Constable Hill was dismissed as being pre-arranged. The main flaw in these suggestions was his meeting with Dwyer which was witnessed by Amelia Blencoe.

For two and a half hours Hunt nervously awaited the jury's verdict. On their return to court they found him guilt on all charged. The judge agreed and sentenced Hunt to two years imprisonment accompanied by hard labour.

Hunt's motives were never really established. Was he employing criminals to thieve on his behalf? Or, was he just setting them up to be arrested to he could claim the reward money? Either way he was abusing his office of constable and finally got his just reward.

6

THE MARTON FIRE

(1853 – Marton)

Superintendent James Isaac of the Knightlow Hundred Police shared the doubts of his colleagues. He looked at what remained of Richard Heath's rickyard. It was unlikely the fire which had destroyed about £1,000 worth of his crops had started accidentally. In particular James was most unhappy about the actions of William Rainbow.

The 21st May 1853 had begun normally at Richard's farm in Marton. Living in Leamington, Richard's farmhouse was occupied by shepherd Thomas Groom and his wife Catherine. She remembered seeing Rainbow sat in the yard eating his breakfast which was most unusual. Soon afterwards he went to start ploughing. When she next looked outside, Catherine was horrified to see smoke coming from the rickyard.

Screaming she ran outside to find Rainbow. Although Catherine could not find him she felt he must have heard her screams, but there was no response from him. When she found him he offered to go to the next village for assistance. Having done so he declined to help fight the fire preferring to go to Leamington and tell Richard what had happened. In spite of having seen several people on the way, Rainbow told nobody about the fire until he met up with Thomas Marriott from Marton who agreed to go to Leamington. Rainbow went home.

Witnesses would say later how totally unconcerned Rainbow appeared to be about the whole incident. There was no sense of urgency about him. He did not return to the farm until later and was accompanied by his father.

Rainbow did not enjoy a good relationship with his employer. His honesty was suspect after he had 'mislaid' one of Richard's sovereigns during a trip to London. Rainbow maintained he had given it to somebody in mistake for a shilling. Also there had been problems concerning his stealing peas from Richard.

The first police officer on the scene was William Darton who was surprised to be asked, by Rainbow, to help move some wood. Rainbow told him how Richard would want to know what help the police had given. Later James Isaac arrived and took charge. A former Metropolitan Police Officer, he was to become the first Chief Constable of the Warwickshire Constabulary four years later. He was assisted by Inspector George Smallbone also from Knightlow. Soon afterwards they were joined by Inspector Field from the Metropolitan Police who was well experienced in fire investigations.

It did not take them long to become very suspicious of Rainbow. Nobody else had been seen anywhere near the rickyard. Then, despite his protests to the contrary, he was found to have a pipe which he smoked at the farm where smoking was forbidden.

On 1 June the coroner opened the inquest at the *Black Horse* in Marton. Normally inquests are only held in cases of sudden death or finding treasure trove. However, the coroner wished to revive the old custom of investigating fires. He needed to establish if there was sufficient evidence to put anybody before the court. Rainbow, who was the prime suspect, was not present when the inquest opened, so the coroner adjourned it until he appeared.

When questioned Rainbow admitted rising before five o'clock, After feeding and grooming the horses he started his breakfast. Normally he ate in the stables but decided to eat in the yard this morning as it was a nice day with the sun shining. However, he denied going near the ricks. Somewhat unwillingly he admitted smoking in the fields but denied doing to in the stables. The question of his smoking was to be a major issue. It became more so after other witnesses reported having seen him smoking in the stables and shortly before the fire.

Faced with this testimony, Rainbow was forced to admit to smoking. Other witnesses testified to hearing him boast about having set fire to the ricks. At this point the inquest was adjourned for a week.

Before the adjournment few people could have doubted Rainbow's guilt. Nothing happened during the following week for their views to change. A suggestion of gypsies being responsible was disproved quickly. Although there were gypsies in the area, none had been seen near Richard's farm.

Evidence was given by Rainbow's father concerning some strangers who had been seen by the fire. Another witness had seen a young boy, but nobody else had seen the strangers. Yet, in spite of all the police enquiries going on, the old man had not approached any police officers with this information. If he had hoped to help his son by this revelation, the opposite was to be the case. Rainbow seemed aware of this and was observed pulling his father's coat whilst the older man testified.

The last part of the evidence concentrated on how much ploughing Rainbow had carried out before being found by Catherine Groom. His estimates were totally discredited by an expert ploughman. He maintained Rainbow could not have ploughed so much land in the time he said he had taken. In fairness he might not have known the time as Marton Church did not possess a clock. The inference being Rainbow had needed the extra time to fire the ricks. Once this crucial evidence was added to the poor relationship he had with Richard, the result seemed fairly obvious.

Summing up the coroner considered Rainbow's having breakfast in the yard as being all part of his act. Throughout the affair Rainbow had been unhelpful in refusing to fight the fire, lying about his smoking activities and times. The jury decided the fire had been started deliberately and Rainbow was the culprit.

The coroner considered he had enough evidence to commit Rainbow for trial at the next Assizes. For some reason he preferred not to do so and left that task to the magistrates. Yet, Rainbow never stood trial. His case was considered by the grand jury who agreed the prosecution was based purely on suspicion. There was no real evidence against him. Consequently they dismissed the charge.

7

VISIT TO BIRMINGHAM

(1854 – Rugby)

Ann Godwin entered her patient's house very quietly by the back door. It was her second visit that morning in November 1854 to the cottage by the old Rugby Railway Station. Knowing the severity of William Voss's mental illness she knew something had happened.

William had been missing and Ann could not get any sense out of his mother Elizabeth and eldest daughter Mary. They had been strangely silent and clearly very frightened. Now Ann crept quietly upstairs and began looking in the bedrooms. In one she found the body of Sarah Ann Voss, William's youngest daughter. She had been stabbed in the throat. There was still no sign of William.

Prior to his illness William had been employed by the London and North Western Railway until just a few weeks earlier. He lived with his mother and Sarah whilst Mary lived nearby. There was no mention made of a wife. As his illness progressed William lost his job. As Ann nursed him she became increasingly concerned about his mental state and believed he was deranged. Her treatment involved using leeches and wrapping his head in vinegar soaked bandages. It was to no avail and William's condition worsened.

He developed a persecution complex believing people were trying to undermine him and his authority. Noises became a problem to him and he could not bear the sound of his mother closing her snuff box.

During October he was examined by John Baker a local surgeon. As his condition worsened Baker found William's pulse to be full and hard. He patient was not sleeping at night and he thought these were all signs of an unspecified brain disease. Yet, in spite of all these afflictions, William was known to be very kind to his daughters, especially Sarah.

Only hours before her death Sarah and Mary had made plans to go to Birmingham for the day. When Sarah told her father he was totally against the idea and would not listen to his daughter's plea. Finally the two of them quarrelled and went to bed in a temper. But William could not sleep. The next morning he looked drawn and ill and was wild eyed. He took Sarah a cup of tea in bed, possibly as a peace gesture, but she refused to drink it. She was still angry with her father.

Just then Mary arrived and went upstairs to see her sister. She found a strained atmosphere in the bedroom and learned quickly how William would not agree to the girls going to Birmingham. Knowing there was no point in arguing with him she went downstairs closely followed by William. Suddenly he ran back upstairs leaving Mary and her grandmother waiting unsure of what to do.

"Oh father!" screamed Sarah. "I will never do so again." Her scream was followed by an ominous silence. Deeply worried Mary ran back upstairs. Thrusting open the door into Sarah's room she saw her father kneeling on the bed. "Oh father!" she cried and pulled him to one side.

"Hold your noise!" he retorted. "I'm not going to hurt her."

Mary was relieved to see nothing in his hands. Later she found a cut on one of her fingers. But her relief was short lived. William's mother came into the room and pulled him off Sarah's bed. It was then both women saw blood on his hands.

"You wicked man!" screamed his mother, "You've killed your daughter."

William agreed adding how he expected to be hanged for it in due course. He promised to give himself up to the police but, in the meantime he ordered them to stay in Sarah's bedroom whilst he went downstairs. But he did not leave the house. Instead he drank some white wine and smoked his pipe. Taking some paper he wrote a letter and put it with his purse which he left on the table. The letter instructed his purse and contents to be given to his nephew. Then he went back upstairs.

Mary and her grandmother clutched each other as they heard his footsteps getting nearer. On entering the room he ordered them both to swear an oath not to tell anybody what had happened that morning. Absolutely terrified they had no choice but to agree. Once they had sworn he made them seal the oath by kissing the Bible. Meekly they continued doing as they were told. Satisfied at last, William went back downstairs. Minutes later they were relived to see him leave the cottage.

Sadly they went downstairs not knowing what to do. They were still in a state of shock when Ann Goodwin found them in her first visit. After finding Sarah's body Ann quickly raised the alarm. Soon a murder hunt was under way led by James Isaac the Chief Constable.

Dr Baker examined Sarah and found a further three wounds in her body. She had bled to death. In spite of making a thorough search of the house, it was some days before the murder weapon was found. Meanwhile William had seemingly disappeared without trace.

Nine days later he was found and arrested in nearby Southam. He continually denied having anything to do with the crime and actually seemed genuinely surprised when charged with Sarah's murder. In due course he stood trial at Warwick Assizes.

Whilst awaiting trial, William was examined by Dr William Parsey from Hatton Asylum. He soon discovered how William suffered from loss of memory and was forever complaining of a bad head. Dr Parsey considered him to be insane and testified accordingly in court. At Sarah's inquest Dr Baker had told the coroner how he considered his patient to be of unsound mind. However, when giving evidence in court he denied ever having made those remarks, maintaining he had initially treated William for an ulcer. William was acquitted of Sarah's murder and was committed to a lunatic asylum for the rest of his life.

Ironically, before losing his job, William had been employed as a railway policeman.

8

THE GALLANT SERGEANT

(1855 – Bedworth)

Sergeant James Harrison waited impatiently as the ship moored. At long last he was back home again in England with the horrors of the Crimean War far away. Thinking the medals, wounds and frostbite, all gained in his Country's service, would entitle him to quite a reception, with squared shoulders he marched proudly off the ship.

Had James realised just what his reception would be, there is little doubt he would have decided to remain in the Crimea. Instead of a hero's welcome, he was arrested on a charge of bigamy concerning his marriage to Mary Pettit. Just a few hours after landing James found himself locked up in Warwick Gaol.

It must be remembered before the Matrimonial Causes Act became law in 1857, divorce could take place only by a private Act of Parliament. Even separation required the sanction of an ecclesiastical or church court. In either case it was a very expensive business and far beyond James's means. To make matters worse any hearing before a church court could go on for years and remarriage was not allowed during this period. Consequently, couples tended to live together or commit bigamy. James chose the latter but not content to have just one wife, he had three all at the same time!

His troubles all began several years earlier when he was serving in India. In Cawnpore he met and married Ann Moon. On their return to England, James enlisted in the Gloucestershire Militia, and moved to Coventry. For some undisclosed reason, he sent Ann to Birmingham. At the same time, he changed his name to William Henry Harrison James.

Whilst living in Coventry he met Mary Eliza Pettit who lived in Leamington Spa. On 1 December 1853 they were married at St Michael's Church in Coventry. The Nuneaton Workhouse Master Henry Churn and Eliza Appletree were witnesses. The only problem was the fact that Harrison's wife, Ann was still alive. As there had been no divorce, in the eyes of the law she remained his lawful wife.

Within two years, Mary had been abandoned for Mary Reader whom James prepared to make his third wife. Ironically Henry Church and Eliza Appletree appeared once more as witnesses to the wedding service which took place in Bedworth in August 1855. Soon afterwards, James was posted to the Crimea to fight against the Russians. He had a hard but distinguished war. By the time he came home he had been awarded four medals with a further ten clasps to them. He was a hero in everybody's eyes.

Whilst in prison, James had a surprise visit from his first wife Ann. She positively identified him to Henry Adkins, Governor of Warwick Gaol. Initially James denied ever knowing her let alone their being man and wife. Overnight he suffered some remorse and next day admitted the truth to Henry Adkins. Gradually the story unfolded and by the time he appeared in Court, James faced two charges if bigamy. His reputation, already fuelled by his war records, grew. When he appeared at the Assizes the court was crowded.

A hush descended on the court room and all eyes focused on James. His entrance into court could not have been staged managed any better. He was an impressive looking man made more so by his uniform and medals. For some reason he was not legally represented and the judge appointed Mr Spooner to undertake the defence.

Spooner's first request was for two separate trials, one for each of the bigamous marriages. The prosecution agreed, being very confident of the successful outcome of the trial. The evidence against James seemed straightforward enough. Henry Churn and Eliza Appletree testified to having witnessed the marriage between James and Mary Pettit. Once the church registers were produced a guilty verdict seemed a foregone conclusion. But Spooner had seen a flaw in the prosecution's case. He argued the prosecution had not proved the first marriage to absolute satisfaction. In the absence of that proof James could not be guilty. The judge agreed and directed the jury to find him not guilty.

The court erupted in total uproar and it took some minutes for calm to be restored. Spooner asked for an adjournment before the second trial so he could study what evidence was available. The judge agreed and the second trial was delayed until later in the week. Once again James pleaded not guilty.

Henry Churn and Eliza Appletree testified again to witnessing James's third marriage. They were followed by another witness to the ceremony – William Reader who was Mary's brother. Undeterred, Spooner sprung his surprise and called Mary Pettit (also known as Mary James) into court. His intention being to show her marriage to James as being illegal. The prosecution objected immediately and a long legal argument began.

The only way Spooner could declare this marriage illegal was to prove the first marriage was legal! But, he had already proved it was not in the first trial. The judge had the final say in the matter and refused to allow her to testify and effectively destroyed Spooner's defence. The only course left was for Spooner to concentrate on his client's past exemplary behaviour. He described the battles in which James had fought and so on. All the while he used expressions life "The gallant Sergeant James Harrison" and regaled the jury with examples of "his kindness and attention to the soldiers under him".

The judge began summing up and was interrupted immediately by the foreman of the jury. It appeared some jurists were unhappy about the authenticity of the two marriage certificates. There can be little doubt they were seeking for ways to acquit James who had the sympathy of the court with him. By now the judge's tolerance was wearing thin and he assured them, in no uncertain terms, the certificates were in order.

Reluctantly the jury had no choice but to convict James on the second charge.

When passing sentence the judge emphasised no injury had been done! Consequently he would only sentence James to two months imprisonment with hard labour. Even then, he would not press the sentence until reviewed by another judge.

James was released on bail, with the High Sheriff putting himself up as surety. Before leaving the Court, he thanked and saluted the judge. It is not known whether or not he ever served his sentence.

9

A WORSE CASE OF MANSLAUGHTER

(1863 – Fenny Compton)

Thomas Ricketts was horrified when he saw his uncle. The elderly man was covered in blood and quite unable to stand without support. He had not expected their pleasant walk to have such a violent ending. No doubt he must have wondered if his own actions had led to his uncle being so cruelly beaten.

Charles Plummer, an elderly retired gentleman's servant, lived quietly with his wife in Broad Street, Warwick. Having no children of his own, Charles took an interest in his nephew's family. On this fateful day 18 October 1863, he went to visit his nephew, Thomas Ricketts a farmer in Fenny Compton. Thomas was also a Parish Constable.

The two men had set off through the fields accompanied by Thomas's small dog. Whilst looking at some animals, two other men appeared on a nearby footpath walking towards them. They were Charles Beere and his younger brother Henry. Both were labourers who lived in nearby Northend and had been drinking.

Thomas's dog ran towards the brothers. It was never suggested he was barking or acting aggressively, but neither brother wanted the dog near them. One of the brothers made an abusive gesture and shouted "Go on!" Whether the gesture and words were meant towards Thomas or the dog was never made clear. But Thomas was clearly offended.

"You go on!" he retorted. Charles Beere retaliated by demanding Thomas's identity. Replying he was a Parish Constable, and owner of the field Thomas added threatening to arrest them for drunkenness if they did not go away. Unfortunately Charles Beere took the reply as a provocation.

Not being a man prepared to ignore such a challenge, he threw off his coat then squared up to Thomas. For a while Henry stood between the two men trying to calm his brother but Charles was in no mood for listening and he punched Thomas a heavy blow on the head. Staggering, Thomas seized his uncle's stick and set about Charles with it. Not content with that, he continued hitting his opponent.

At this point his uncle intervened, and begged his nephew to stop hitting the other man. Thomas paused and Charles took advantage of the respite, regained his feet and recommenced his attack. In retaliation the stick flashed again and again. Suddenly it broke and Thomas lost the advantage. For a white both men rolled on the ground with Thomas gaining the upper hand until Henry Beere went to his brother's rescue. Scrambling to his feet Thomas ran from the field, leaving his uncle behind, little realising what was to happen next.

Running towards Fenny Compton, he met his cousin William Ricketts and quickly explained what had happened. William ran towards the field whilst Thomas went home cleaned himself up and sent a small boy for the police.

When Thomas next saw his uncle it was obvious the old man had been severely beaten. He had his uncle taken indoors and went with Constable John Oughton after the Beere brothers and arrested them about half a mile from the scene.

Loading the brothers into a cart, the constables set off towards Southam. On the way, Charles tried to bribe Thomas to go easy on him. Totally incensed, Thomas diverted the cart to his house and he took the prisoners inside to see the pathetic state Charles Plummer was in. The brothers cried when they saw him.

Resuming their journey to Southam, Constable Oughton overheard Henry blaming his brother for not listening to him and giving the old man a good kicking. Later there would be much legal wrangling over the admissibility of this evidence. Constable Oughton took possession of one of Charles Beere's boots which had hairs sticking to it! They matched the colour of those on the old man's head.

Tragically Charles Plummer died two days later. An autopsy on his body revealed severe bruising to his chest, three broken ribs, cut eyes and severe head injuries. The examining surgeon agreed the injuries could have been caused by a boot. Having been in a healthy state until then, the cause of his death was given as being injuries to the brain.

When Inspector James Gaskins broke the new of the old man's death to the Beere brothers, he cautioned them against replying. Ignoring the advice Henry put the blame firmly on his brother who agreed.

The inquest at the *Red Lion* in Fenny Compton aroused much local interest, but little extra evidence came to light. Whilst testifying Inspector Gaskins came into conflict with the Coroner, Mr W Savage Poole, concerning the brothers' confession at the police station.

"You will find if you look at the judge's order..." said the Inspector. "I do not wish to hear the law from you, Mr Gaskins, unless you will take my position and responsibility altogether," interrupted the Coroner. Turning to the jury he added, "You must take your law from me."

As expected they returned a verdict of wilful murder, and the Beere brothers were committed for trial at Warwick Assizes. They appeared there later that year in December.

Following the end of the evidence, the defence entered a plea to have the charge reduced from murder to manslaughter. It was argued there was no malice on the brothers' part. Much was made of Thomas's over reaction and the violence he used. The judge agreed and immediately instructed the jury to find them not guilty. Charles was not so fortunate and the judge soon found him guilty of manslaughter. Describing the act as "A worse case of manslaughter I cannot perceive." The judge sentenced him to penal servitude for life.

Why the old man was attacked remains a mystery. He had not taken part in the fight as far as we know. Perhaps he had said something or was he just in the wrong place at the wrong time. He was not brought back to Warwick but was buried in Fenny Compton Churchyard.

Twenty three years later, another infamous crime at Fenny Compton hit the headlines. This was the murder of Police Constable William Hine.

10
RIGHT OF WAY
(1864 – Brailes)

"I'm determined!" shouted a thoroughly enraged George Ditton. "I'll fix you this time."

It was an unfortunate choice of words which would be remembered for a long time by those who heard them. They were words which lost nothing in their meaning each time they were repeated.

Moments earlier burly gamekeeper George Ditton had stared in disbelief at his arch enemy Henry Clifton who was calmly walking along the disputed footpath, ignoring commands to stop. Shifting his gun to a more comfortable position, George went to challenge him.

George was employed by Henry Sheldon in Brailes. Gamekeepers were not particularly popular and George was no exception. If they were injured in the course of their duties, they could expect to receive little or no sympathy. But, it a poacher was injured, then the keeper responsible would need all the support he could get from his employers to keep him out of court. Recently Henry Sheldon had taken the provocative and unsuccessful step of closing a footpath over his land which had been in use for many years.

It was one of George's jobs to deter trespassers and suspected poachers from using this path. Mr Sheldon hoped George's burly build would be enough to deter people. Henry Clifton, however, was not easily frightened. Only 29 years old, he had quite a formidable reputation in the locality. In January 1864 he had been fined for assaulting George. One month later, the evening of 18 February, Henry was walking along the footpath when he was aware of being seen and challenged by George. He chose to ignore the game-keeper's commands to stop.

Running after him, George grabbed his shoulder demanding to search him. In reply Henry set about the gamekeeper with a stout stick. Taken by surprise, George slipped onto a hand and a knee, but still held the gun in his left hand. Suddenly there was a bang and Henry staggered backwards having been shot in the chest. Falling, he commended his soul to God and died.

In the stunned silence which followed, Thomas Walker appeared and ran straight to the fallen man, but he was too late. Even as Thomas looked at him, he was aware of George complaining about being ignored, with all attention going to the dead man. Thomas was an important witness. Not only did he hear George's threats but also witnessed the actual shooting. He was adamant George had not put the gun to his shoulder before firing, which tended to support the view of the shooting having been accidental. Still ignored, George went home where he was later arrested.

The inquest opened two days later and was held at the *George Inn* at Brailes. As tempers were running very high Police Sergeant John Galloway wisely kept George in custody at Shipston-on-Stour throughout the hearing. At the end of the day the verdict was wilful murder by a majority of 12-3.

Two days later George appeared before the magistrates at the *George Inn* at Shipston-on-Stour. The problems encountered by the police at the inquest were nothing compared with what was to follow. Superintendent James Thompson pleaded for urgent reinforcements. Feelings against George were running so high that the Brailes residents actually paid for his prosecution. The vicar of Brailes preached about the affair and opened a subscription for Henry's mother. Over £20 was raised in the following weeks.

As George was led into court, he was greeted by a loud chorus of boos and hisses. No doubt he was surprised to see his employer sitting as one of the examining magistrates. Mr Lane represented George and soon realised he would have to work hard for his money. Much of the first day's evidence concerned the footpath and whether it was private or not. After evidence had been produced about the animosity between the two men, George had to be removed by the back door to avoid the angry crowd. When the case resumed the crowds were even bigger. Superintendent Thompson gratefully accepted several local tradesmen who volunteered to be special constables. By now well over 1,000 people, in an ugly mood, congregated around the George. Witnesses were obliged to enter and leave court by a window as they could not get through the door. Shouts of "Hang him!" and "Shoot him!" greeted George's arrival.

Mr Lane quoted from the Beere case, the previous year, claiming his client had responded in retaliation to the blows he was receiving. Superintendent Thompson testified to the injuries George had received especially to his shoulder. "Was that why he had been unable to raise the gun to his shoulder before firing!" asked Mr Lane. Cries of derision greeted his pleas to have the charge reduced to manslaughter. A surprise witness was Mr Sheldon who stepped down from the bench and entered the witness box. He maintained it was a private footpath and had given order to stop trespassers. Having given his evidence he resumed his seat with the other magistrates.

Finally Mr Lane won his argument for reducing the charge. No doubt some of the magistrates would have been landowners themselves and there were important issues at stake. George was committed in custody to await trail for manslaughter.

Once George had been removed, peace returned to Brailes and Shipston as the inhabitants settled down in anticipation of a lively trial in the not too distant future. They had little doubt George Ditton would get his just deserts. They were to be disappointed. Whether George would have been found guilty or not must remain a matter of conjecture. In the eyes of the Brailes inhabitants he was guilty of murder and always would be. But it was never put to the test.

On 16 July 1864 at the beginning of the mid-summer Assizes as Warwick, a simple announcement was made. George Ditton had died in prison whilst awaiting trial and there could not be any court hearing. The cause of his death was not revealed.

11

SWEET'S DOG

(1864 – Grendon)

In the darkness Edward Radford woke with a start, wondering if he had been dreaming. Lying still in his bed he strained his ears and listened. The sound came again. It was a definite call for help from someone who sounded badly hurt.

Edward climbed out of bed and threw on some clothes. He remembered looking at the clock and saw it was 3.30 am on a chilly morning in October 1864. Cautiously he went out in the direction of the cries and found the badly beaten John Rowell. Slowly John told his story and soon a full scale search was in operation.

Earlier that evening two local miners, Henry Asher and James Atkins decided to go poaching for rabbits on land at Grendon. Needing a dog, they arranged with George Sweet to borrow his. What they did not realise at the time was the animal was well known in the locality for being a poacher's dog. Poaching any sort of game has long been a problem for landowners. Harsh game laws had been enacted over the centuries to protect landowners' assets. But for determined men like Asher and Atkins, the law held no fear. Gamekeepers were their natural enemies and confrontations usually ended in bloodshed. Neither side asked for quarter nor expected any. This night was to be such an incident.

Asher and Atkins met in Atherstone where they had several drinks before ending up in the *White Hart.* Here they were joined by William Cooke and William Wood. Soon after 11 p.m. four men and Sweet's dog were seen by the level crossing. Two of them were recognised as being Atkins and Cooke.

Meanwhile, Charles Ashley and John Rowell, gamekeepers to Sir

George Chetwynd, were watching for poachers in Big Wood Field at nearby Grendon. Each man carried a stout stick for protection. Suddenly they heard a rabbit squeal and Sweet's dog appeared nearby. Knowing the poachers would not be far behind, gripping their sticks more firmly and with all senses alert, they followed the dog into a clearing where they found some rabbit nets.

As they watched four men appeared. The gamekeepers moved out of cover and challenged the men. Without any warning a stone flew through the air striking John on his forehead. Badly dazed he fell to the ground vaguely aware of Charles fighting for his life nearby. Although he put up a good fight Charles was no match for his two opponents. Wood and Cooke had run away the moment they were challenged.

Soon Charles was on the ground as well being kicked by Asher and Atkins. He vaguely heard one of them shout, "Let's kill the b......" then lost consciousness. Having finished with Charles, the poachers turned their attention on John and began kicking him unconscious.

Some time elapsed before John recovered enough to move and establish he had been blinded in the attack. After a while he gave up calling for Charles as his cries remained unanswered. Unable to stand he started to crawl away calling for help. Somehow he made his way to Edward Radford's cottage before his cries were heard.

Almost an hour and a half later, the unfortunate Charles was found where he had been thrown. Nearby the searchers found part of a rusty coloured coat. Once he regained consciousness Charles told his listeners what had happened. In particular one of his assailants had been wearing a rusty coloured coat, but more importantly he had recognised Sweet's dog. By now the police had been called. Soon all four men were in custody, strongly denying the allegations. However, any doubts the police might have had were dispelled when it was found the stone which struck John had come from the nearby railway. In fact it matched the ballast used at the same level crossing where the four men had been seen.

John and Charles recovered slowly. Charles was clearly badly affected by his beating. He lost his confidence and became very hesitant in his manner and speech.

In early December 1864 all four stood trial at Warwick Assizes. The judge agreed there should be two separate trials. There would be the attempted murder of John Rowell and the assault on Charles Ashley. The poaching charges were dropped and the prisoners pleaded not guilty to the others.

They had no real defence. Several witnesses had seen them all together with Sweet's dog. The most damning evidence came from Ann Green who used to live with Asher, but had left him after his arrest.

She remembered Asher coming home at about two o'clock that morning. He was wearing a different coat and there was a very noticeable wound to one of his eyes. When she pressed him for an explanation he explained about the fight but was fairly confident he had not been recognised. He told her the sale of the rabbits had been arranged with the proceeds to be shared out later. As it happened, Mrs Atkins bought one of them. Finally he told Ann there was nothing to worry about, but was arrested soon afterwards.

All the defence could do was attack the credibility of the witness. Poor Charles was criticised for the hesitant way he gave his evidence. As for Ann, she was derided for having 'peached' on her man. Not that it did much good as the jury took just forty-five minutes to reach their verdicts.

Wood and Cooke were acquitted, but Asher and Atkins were found guilty. They suffered a similar verdict in the second trial.

Asher and Atkins pleaded with the judge for mercy. Both claimed they were as innocent as newly born children. It was not the best of ideas. For the benefit of the court the judge quoted their criminal records.

Asher had nine previous convictions for theft, night poaching, assault and wilful damage. Atkins had a lesser record, but it included one conviction for armed trespass. Clearly the judge was not impressed with their pleas of innocence.

He sentenced Asher to fifteen years penal servitude and Atkins to ten years.

12

A GLASS OF BEER

(1866 – Stoneleigh)

Frank Wells leapt angrily to his feet as he felt the cold liquid hit his back. Turning quickly he glared at the laughing soldiers behind him. He was far from amused and could find nothing to laugh about. Their laughing only made him more angry.

Moments earlier he had been sitting in the beer tent cutting up cheese with his clasp knife. Suddenly a glass of beer had been tipped down his back. Still clutching his knife, Wells began arguing with them. Whether the beer had been spilt accidentally or otherwise was never established. It was unlikely to have made any difference even if it had been an accident. With his tormentors in such a quarrelsome frame of mind they reacted quickly to the other man's anger. The laughter stopped abruptly and their eyes hardened as they shouted back at him. Ever mindful of the knife they took great care to keep out of its range. Neither party showed any inclination to back down.

The day of the Annual Military Prize Shooting Competition at Stoneleigh Deer Park had passed peacefully enough on that July day in 1866 until the end of the contest when the beer tents were opened for the soldiers. In the general melee around the bar, it was inevitable some beer would have been spilt. But Wells did not see the spillage this way. He took it as a personal affront. Being a volunteer in the Leamington Militia he was soon supported by friends, and continued waving the knife to emphasise his point of view.

The beer tent keeper, Mr Butler, was no coward and determined to stop the fracas before if developed further. After taking the precautionary step of first sending for police assistance, he pulled Wells to one side and advised him to put the knife away. Knowing the knife gave him the advantage, Wells made it clear he had no intention of surrendering it to anybody. Realising the futility of trying to convince the man, Mr Butler moved away and waited impatiently for the police.

By the time Constable John Stonehill arrived more soldiers had gathered around to watch and shout encouragement. As their numbers grew, everybody surged out of the tent. Mr Butler would testify later how they nearly all seemed the worse for drink. The constable waded into the middle of the throng and demanded to know what was happening.

In reply several of the soldiers shouted, "This b...... has been using his knife!" Turning to Wells, the constable demanded the surrender of the knife. Feigning injured innocence Wells denied any knowledge of having such a weapon. "I have not got a knife", was all he said repeatedly.

Keeping his temper, the constable replied, "I can see it in your hand." Wells refused to hand it over.

As often happens in this type of situation the constable quickly found himself being looked upon as the villain, and accused of persecuting the 'innocent' soldier. John continued demanding to take possession of the knife and was acutely aware how the mood of the soldiers had changed against him. Wells steadfastly denied having a knife although it was plainly visible to all, but now he started to close it. He did so clumsily and managed to cut his hand in the process before dropping the knife.

The blood on his hand excited the nearest soldiers who saw it. They shouted to the others and blamed John for causing the injury. With a growl of anger, the mob surged towards the unhappy constable.

Surrounded by over 100 angry men, John was relieved to see Inspectors John Lapworth and John Galloway push their way towards him. They were followed closely by another two or three constables. For a moment all went quiet and the atmosphere remained very tense. Then a bottle flew through the air and hit one of the constables. It was the signal for the pushing, shouting and swearing to be resumed.

Meanwhile, news of the riot had spread like wildfire throughout the park with many of the remaining soldiers running to the scene. Amongst them were several of their own officers. First to arrive was Colour Sergeant Squires who had the advantage of being mounted. A quick thinking man, he realised instant action was necessary. Without any hesitation he rode straight into a group of Warwick Volunteers. Frightened by all the noise and moving bodies, his horse began kicking out and hit several rioters. They reacted angrily by turning their attention towards the unfortunate rider and tried to pull him out of the saddle.

Other militia officers now tried to pacify their men but it was a futile effort. The soldiers, no doubt encouraged by the beer they had consumed, were in no mood to listen. One of the ringleaders, a Private named Prestidge, was determined to continue attacking the police officers. However, he was well known to Inspector Lapworth who easily recognised him. As well as trying to cope with the shouting and pushing soldiers, the police now faced a new danger from the barrage of missiles being thrown at them.

Lapworth was struck twice and another missile damaged John Stonehill's hat. He had joined the Warwickshire Constabulary in July 1866 and was to leave the following year. Heavily outnumbered the future was looking bleak for the police and Sergeant Squires. Suddenly the sounds of a bugle could be heard above the shouting. The soldiers stopped fighting as their training took over and they began to assemble in their companies away from the beer tent. Once peace and quiet had been restored, Wells and Prestidge were arrested by the Inspectors and handed over to the Military for punishment.

A Military Court of Enquiry was later convened under Major Macken during which it was suggested bayonets had been used in the riot. This allegation was strongly denied; likewise accusations about Galloway trying to choke Wells. The Inspector agreed he had gripped the man's collar but only to restrain him. Having been found guilty Lance Corporal Mann was fined £2 and Privates Green, Hardman, Prestidge and Underhill £1. All were dismissed from the militia.

13
CRIME OF PASSION
(1872 – Priors Hardwick)

"Walter!" screamed Betsy Handcock. "Walter! He's cutting me!"

Downstairs thirteen year old Walter Handcock listened, terrified, to his stepmother's screams. Although he was accustomed to the fights between his father and stepmother, somehow tonight seemed different. Knowing he was no match for his father, Walter fled into the night to find help.

Betsy was Edward Handcock's third wife. She lived with him and their four children in Priors Hardwick. A butcher by trade, Edward had been insanely jealous of his wives and poor Betsy was no exception. Matters came to a head on the night of 13 November 1872.

Walter had come home from work as normal but whilst eating his tea, he was aware of Betsy going out of the house. He was slightly surprised she had not said where she was going. Meanwhile he could hear his father in the kitchen busy sharpening a knife. However, Walter was relieved to see Edward had left the knife behind when he went upstairs.

Half an hour later Betsy returned and was clearly agitated. To Edward's twisted mind she had gone to see her lover. Only much later would the real reason for her absence be explained. Her mission had not been successful. Slowly she undressed the three smaller children and prepared them for bed. Unable to delay any longer she took them slowly upstairs. Passing Walter she muttered "I expect there'll be a fillelew when I get upstairs."

As she finished putting the last child to bed, Edward appeared suddenly from out of the back room. Even as she realised he had a knife in his hand, she was stabbed in each arm in quick succession. Then Edward stabbed her in the thigh twisting the knife as he did so. Betsy fell back onto the spare bed, screaming for help.

Her cries were heard by next door neighbour Hannah Hart. The adjoining cottage walls were very thin and she had heard the Handcocks fighting many times before, but not like tonight. She ran outside and met Walter. Together they went back to Betsy's house.

They found her lying at the foot of the stairs in the hallway in a pool of her own blood. Hannah sent Walter for a doctor and began to comfort Betsy. In due course she was carried back upstairs whilst the doctor treated her. But he could not stop the bleeding from Betsy's thigh and she died later that evening watched by Hannah and Walter.

Meanwhile Edward made no attempt to escape but remained there until the Parish Constable, William Sharpe arrived to be greeted by Edward confessing to having stabbed his wife and gloating about having done it in spite of her hiding his knives. Sharpe was relieved when Police Sergeant Thomas Webb arrived and arrested Edward. He merely commented, "It is all this whoring," as they took him away.

Later Webb returned to the cottage and made a preliminary search hoping to find the murder weapon. He was unsuccessful but managed to find the sharpening steel. Convinced it was still there, he returned next morning. This time his diligence was rewarded and the bloodstained knife was found on a window sill. Strangely, it had been covered in cobwebs overnight.

It was common knowledge in the village how Edward was obsessed in his belief Betsy had been having affairs with every man she met. In particular he blamed a man called Warren who was never identified. Sadly his neighbours made matters worse by teasing him all the time. To make matters worse, he had started drinking heavily. Only the day before Betsy's death, Edward had been complaining to the vicar about her antics. Trying to convince him of the real truth the vicar thought Edward was drunk.

In reality Betsy was a very quiet and respectable woman who rarely went out. There was never any evidence to suggest any infidelity on her part. It was all in Edward's mind. Tragically on the night of her death, Betsy had gone out desperately trying to find a police officer to give her protection. Sadly she had not been able to find one.

As England has never embraced the principle of a "Crime of Passion" Edward found himself charged with murder. He appeared at Warwick Assizes just before Christmas 1872 where he pleaded not guilty.

The prosecution evidence was fairly brief, but very much to the point. Medical evidence was produced to show Betsy's wounds could not have been self inflicted. There was nothing the defence could do until Edward's eldest daughter Eliza was called as a witness. Little Eliza, only six years old, climbed into the witness box and cried throughout the entire proceedings. The nature of the oath was explained to her and she was duly sworn! Just how much she really understood is a matter of conjecture. She explained how her father had "slipped the knife in".

The defence seized on this point immediately. They accused her having been primed in what to say in court. They failed miserably as little Eliza bravely kept to her story.

As a forlorn hope they tried to prove Betsy's infidelities as being the cause of her death. This attack failed as well. They would have done better to have concentrated on Edward's insanity.

Edward remained impassive throughout, even when the jury took just two minutes to find him guilty. He seemed completely oblivious even when the judge sentenced him to death before his removal from the court.

With Christmas being so close, his execution was delayed until the new year. During this period attempts were made to have him reprieved, but without success. On 7 January 1873, the hangman arrived to carry out his duties.

Although executions no longer took place in public, a huge crowd gathered outside the new Warwick prison and waited expectantly. In due course they heard the sound of the trap door being opened. Soon afterwards a black flag was unfurled over the prison. Edward's miserable life was ended.

14

POSSESSED BY WITCHES

(1875 – Long Compton)

Ann Tennant cowered in terror at John Haywood's feet. One look at his face told her she could expect no mercy. He was determined to kill her. She saw him raise his pitchfork and screamed as he stabbed her once more.

Forty-five years old John was renowned in Long Compton for having a violent nature which had worsened since falling out of a tree and injuring his head. Whilst be blamed witchcraft for keeping him out of work, the truth was nobody wanted the responsibility of employing such a violent man on a regular basis. Only when no other labour was available would anyone employ him. Such was the case on 15 September 1875 when John was employed to carry out some fieldwork. All day he had raved on about the witches in the village. His views were well known and shared by some of the villagers, including his parents. They never left their cottage doors unlocked even if only going to the coal shed. John had always considered elderly Ann Tennant to be one of the many witches in Long Compton. He had sworn to kill them all! To make matters worse, Ann was his next door neighbour. A clash was inevitable and it came as John returned home from work.

For most of the day John's fellow workers had ignored him, having heard his ravings before. They were probably slightly scared of him. However, young Henry Evans walked home with him to Long Compton. John carried his bottle and jacket in one hand and his pitchfork in the other.

During the day Ann had been out visiting her family. On going home she realised there was no bread in the house and went out

43

again to buy some. Returning home she had the misfortune to meet up with her neighbour. Immediately he saw her, John dropped everything except the pitchfork which he took from his shoulder and pointed at Ann. Making loud unintelligible noises he charged at the defenceless woman.

Although very sprightly for her 80 years, Ann never stood a chance against the comparatively younger man. He chased after Ann continually stabbing her in the back and legs with the pitchfork. Suddenly she tripped and fell but John kept up his murderous attack. All the time he shouted about ridding Long Compton of its witches.

John Taylor heard the screams. Running to investigate he saw Ann being stabbed. He was well aware of John's violent temper and reputation but still tried to help her. Somehow he took the pitchfork off John as other people arrived. Some held on to John whilst others carried Ann home and sent for Dr Nicholson from nearby Chipping Norton. He found her bleeding profusely from puncture wounds in the head and legs. As her varicose veins had been punctured, he could not stop the bleeding and she died about 11.00 p.m. The cause of her death was given as haemorrhage and shock.

Meanwhile John had been arrested by Police Constable John Simpson, and made no attempt to deny what he had done. "No odds about it." was his reply on being arrested. "I hope she is dead. There is a lot I will serve the same." Even when charged with Ann's murder, he remained totally indifferent to the whole proceedings.

Whilst in Warwick Gaol awaiting trial, John's behaviour was most bizarre. He never accepted he had done anything wrong and quoted regularly from the Bible to prove his point. Finally John produced what he considered to be the unequivocal proof of his being possessed by witches. His audience was clearly surprised when he produced a phial of urine with a bubble floating in it. It was his urine and the bubble was the proof! It was obvious the man was seriously ill.

His trial at Warwick Assizes was really a formality. The defence argued strongly to have the charge reduced to one of manslaughter, but the judge disagreed. He was adamant all the facts needed hearing.

John must have presented a pathetic figure in the dock. As if his mental state was not a sufficient enough handicap, congenital deafness affected his speech. He gave the impression of being a typical village idiot. All the medical witnesses agreed he was not responsible for his actions. In their opinion nothing could have prevented John from killing Ann. It was a crime waiting to happen.

The jury debated the facts for only a few minutes before agreeing with the doctors. They found John not guilty on grounds of insanity. He was committed to a mental asylum for the rest of his life.

Following the trial, the judge gave a homily about the whole question of witchcraft being practised in South Warwickshire. His recommendations were that such beliefs were now outdated and had no place in modern society. Thus the sad case of John Haywood and Ann Tennant passed into history where it was to lie dormant for the next 70 years.

On 14 February 1945 Charles Walton was found murdered in a field at the foot of Meon Hill in Lower Quinton, not far away from Long Compton. He was a farm labourer and one of the weapons used was his own two pronged pitchfork. The murder had all the appearances of being a ritualistic killing. Not surprisingly it did not take long for tales of witchcraft, including John Haywood's case, to surface once more.

Detective Superintendent Robert Fabian from Scotland Yard headed the murder enquiry at the request of the Chief Constable. After he had been shown a report of Ann's murder, and other black magic tales in the area, he took the provocative and often ridiculed step of stating publicly how witchcraft could have been a contributory factor in Walton's murder. Whether or not Fabian believed in sorcery is debatable but using this ploy was a media coup. Furthermore it enabled him to keep their interest in his enquiry for a long time.

Sadly none of these tactics worked and Charles Walton's murder still remains unsolved.

15

THE HATTERS' RIOTS

(1878 – Mancetter)

The police heaved a sigh of relief as they saw the angry crowds move away from Mr Stafford's house. For the most part their mood had been peaceful. But Superintendent Henry Walker was sadly mistaken if he thought that was the end of the matter. It was just the beginning.

Some days earlier, in late June 1878, the owners of the exclusive Atherstone based hat manufacturers of Messrs Wilson and Stafford, had made an unexpected and unpopular announcement. There was to be a general reduction in wages! The news was received with a mixture of disbelief and anger. Sixteen workers reacted by resigning immediately. The next few days saw an uneasy calm settle over the company and local community. It could not be described as a happy atmosphere.

By 26 June the workers were in an ugly mood, with some going on strike. Their main hatred was directed against Messrs Wilson and Stafford personally. Rightly believing violence was not very far away, the two hatters went to the police. Fortunately Superintendent Walker took their fears seriously and some eight constables were drafted into the two men's houses. Later that same day a large crowd gathered outside Mr Stafford's house in a fairly peaceful demonstration which let him know they were far from happy with his management of the company.

The next day passed in a state of uneasy calm with an air of expectation all over Atherstone. Everywhere people waited to see what would happen next. Towards dusk a large crowd of 40 or more gathered before marching back to Mr Stafford's house once more.

They were led by Samuel Shilton who wore a mask and rode on a donkey. He was ably supported by Frederick Webb and Charles Turvey. Once outside their employer's house, they began a barrage of shouting, whistling, catcalling and howling, all directed at Mr Stafford.

Acting on instructions from the police, he did not show himself. After about half an hour, the mob became bored and began showering the house with a vast array of missiles. Luckily nobody was hurt and the damage was minimal. Having exhausted their ammunition, the mob began to drift away. As they did so Walker realised they were moving towards their next target, Mr Wilson's house in nearby Mancetter. Gathering his officers together quickly, Walker moved them all to Mancetter, arriving just before the rioters. But it was a far different mob to the one they had just seen.

By now it was some 1500 strong. Mr and Mrs Wilson and their seven children were absolutely terrified and hid at the rear of their house. The police officers knew there was little they could do to stop the rioters. Nervously and watched by his pitifully few men, Superintendent Walker went to talk to the mob and its leaders. When they seemed to be listening to him, Walker became hopeful of a peaceful settlement. But it was not to be as George Joyce interrupted him shouting, "Don't go home at all! I know the law as well as they do!" George Baker agreed with him excitedly. Shilton stepped in and took over the leadership. "Let's have him out" he cried, "Let's have the house down and dress the bricks!"

The mob roared its approval completely drowning out Walker's final plea. With an ever increasing roar they surged forward. Ignoring the few police officers, they pushed through the hedge and onto some high ground in the garden. Henry Chetwin urged them to "Bring your catapults!" They needed no second invitation. A steady stream of missiles of all types hit Mr Wilson's house breaking several windows. Powerless to act the hapless police could only stand and watch but they did not waste their time. Later they were able to identify many of the ringleaders.

When the barrage stopped at last, the mob moved away but did not disperse. Horrified the police realised they were heading for the hat manufactory itself, where they caused even more damage before finally going home.

In the quiet aftermath of the riots, Walker began making fresh plans. His first priority was to arrange for reinforcements. In the days that followed large numbers of extra police were drafted into the area. As peace slowly returned to Atherstone, the rioting ringleaders were identified and warrants issued for their arrests.

In due course the 10 main ringleaders appeared at Warwick Assizes. With the exception of Edward Mountford and Henry Thompson they all pleaded guilty to charges of having riotously and tumultuously assembled together to the disturbance of the public peace and, unlawfully, and with force damaged the windows of a house belonging to William Wilson. The whole affair had aroused a considerable interest and there was no shortage of spectators in court.

In his closing address the defence barrister told the judge that numerous gentlemen from Atherstone wished to testify on behalf of the defendants. He added it was their intention to persuade the judge to treat them leniently. It was not a wise choice of words and they were misunderstood by the judge. He took great exception to any suggestion of outsiders trying to influence his decision. On seeing the judge's anger, the barrister went to great lengths to explain what he really meant. The gentlemen had come to give evidence of the accused men's previous good character.

At last the time came for the judge to pass sentence and he started by talking about the dispute. He could find nothing wrong in workers resigning voluntarily is such cases. It was an acceptable way of protesting. But, he argued, taking the law into ones own hands was definitely not! Shilton and Chetwin had been the main instigators of the riot. They each received a three month prison sentence. Joyce received two months. The others went to prison for one month. All sentences included hard labour.

Once the prisoners had been removed, the judge praised the way in which Superintendent Walker and his men had handled the affair. His comments were echoed by the Chief Constable in his next Quarterly Reports.

James Ravenall in Superintendent's uniform.
He was an Inspector in 1895 and investigated the Aston Abortionist.
(Photograph - Courtesy of Warwickshire Constabulary History Society)

Barrack Street, Warwick.
Site of public executions until the new prison was opened.
The rings for holding a rope barrier to restrain
the crowds can still be seen in the wall.
(Photograph - Author)

*The George Inn, Shipston-on-Stour where George Ditton
was committed for trial at Warwick Assizes in 1864
(Photograph - Author)*

III

The churchyard at Kineton where Robert Rudland
fought with John Hutchinson in 1887.
(Photograph - Author)

Warwick Crown Court, formerly where the Assizes and Quarter Sessions sat.
(Photograph - Author)

Warwick Constabulary Headquarters from 1888 - 1948. Nearby the body of James Russell was found in 1892. (Photograph - Courtesy of Warwickshire Constabulary History Society)

The Gardener's Arms in Solihull where Thomas Gateley was shot in 1880.
(Photograph - Courtesy of Solihull Metropolitan Borough Council Education, Libraries and Arts Dept.)

Police Constable Harby Ford (first on left in front row) who was responsible for having Marion Humphries prosecuted in 1892. (Photograph - Courtesy of Warwickshire Constabulary History Society)

16
THE BROTHERS
(1878 – Birdingbury)

M r Neale, landlord of *The Boat* public house at Birdingbury Wharf, was in no mood for practical jokers. He had not long retired to bed and did not take kindly to the frantic hammering on his door. Ignoring the knocking and anguished cries for help, he told his tormentors to go away and went back to bed.

Outside Daniel Cleaver and Edward Goode did not know what else to do. They did not have to be doctors to know their friend Frederick Fletcher was seriously injured. He needed immediate help as they could not stop the flow of blood, clearly he was in danger of bleeding to death. After a brief discussion Daniel ran home to fetch his father and Frederick's mother whilst Edward tried again to rouse the landlord.

During the early evening of 26 September 1878, Frederick's elder brother Edward, had gone to *The Boat* for a drink. Some 11 years older than Frederick he was married with three children, employed locally as a labourer and lived nearby. Frederick still lived at home with his mother in Broadwell about a mile and half from the Inn.

Knowing her eldest son was in *The Boat*, Mrs Fletcher had asked Frederick to go and give him a message from her. He agreed readily and sometime after 7.00 p.m. walked over to Birdingbury. On the way he met Daniel Cleaver who was also going for a drink. It was 7.45 p.m. by the time they arrived and joined Edward Goode who was already in the bar.

Frederick gave the message to his brother, but he could see Edward was not in his usual mood but very quarrelsome. All four stayed drinking in the bar for the evening. Frederick and his friends were still sober at closing time, but Edward Fletcher was well under the influence of alcohol and had left earlier. Nobody was sorry to see him go.

In fact the evening had been marred by Edward. Normally the two brothers enjoyed a good relationship with each other, but not on this night. As Mrs Fletcher testified later, there had been an argument over some incident from several years earlier whereby Edward had suffered some slight at his brother's hands. This had been accompanied by some 'jangling' which was, no doubt, aggravated by drink. As they started home, just outside the Inn, Edward Flecther reappeared.

By now he was in a very aggressive mood and looking for a fight. Without wasting any time he quickly knocked down Edward Goode before turning his full attention to Frederick. He ignored Daniel. Lying dazed on the ground Edward Goode was aware the fight had now moved out of his sight and was some 10 yards away. Suddenly, Frederick reappeared with his right arm bleeding copiously. "Dan!" he cried, "He has done it now. He has cut my arm off."

At first the friends tried to walk Frederick home, but he has lost too much blood and collapsed. It was then they had tried to rouse Mr Neale for help. After Daniel left the scene Edward went back to the Inn. This time he succeeded in convincing Mr Neale of the urgency of the situation. Together they carried Frederick into the bar and tried to force some brandy down him. Sadly it was too late. Frederick was already dead and there was no sign of his brother.

In due course Dr William Lattey arrived from Southam and confirmed Frederick was dead. On further examination of the body he found Frederick had an incised wound in his right arm which had severed the artery and veins. Clearly a knife had been used. The cause of death was soon established as loss of blood. In the doctor's opinion Frederick might have survived if some attempt had been made to bandage the wound.

Meanwhile Police Constable William Wait, from Stockton, had gone to try and find Edward. He was unsuccessful as unbeknown to anyone, the fugitive had gone back home to his mother. She must have persuaded him not to run away. Consequently he waited with her at Broadwell until Constable Wait found him at about 5.30 a.m. He arrested Edward and took him away without a struggle. At the first available opportunity he searched his prisoner and found a bloodstained knife.

Later Edward was charged with his brother's murder by Inspector Jesse Welch who had been at Southam for the past two years. Edward merely replied, "Very good, Sir."

Whilst waiting for Edward's trial to begin the Coroner had carried out his own investigation into Frederick's death. Having heard all the evidence, he was of the opinion the more appropriate charge would be manslaughter. His opinion was accepted by the prosecution and the charge against Edward was reduced.

When Edward appeared at Warwick Assizes in November the same year, he pleaded not guilty to the charge of manslaughter. From the outset it was accepted he had not intended to kill his brother. The main weakness in his defence was his denial of having used the knife to stab Frederick. When the fight started outside *The Boat,* Edward had been carrying a load of broken crockery in a bag on his back and his defence was quite simple. Frederick must have cut himself on a piece of it during the fight. It was a plausible enough defence but he could not explain away the bloodstained knife. It weakened his case so much that the jury did not believe him. After a retirement of only 45 minutes, they found him guilty.

Before passing sentence, the judge harangued Edward, but his message was meant for a wider audience. The degree of provocation was immaterial. Even if there was no intention to use it. There was not justification for anybody to use a knife in a fight. He finished by sentencing Edward to 10 years penal servitude.

17

TRIED AS AND ENGLISHMAN

(1880 – Solihull)

"Jack! I want a word with you!" panted Inspector Stephen Hall one morning in 1885. His words brought a manhunt to a close after nearly five years.

On 3 December 1880, when cowman Thomas Gateley returned to his lodgings in Yardley, near Solihull, he was told about a visitor to his landlady. Curious at first, he quickly became worried when she described the strange man to him. He knew only one such man with a sandy beard and moustache who wore a long Ulster coat and billycock hat. That man could only mean trouble. The stranger did not return to the house.

Two days later, Thomas was having a quiet drink at the *Gardeners Arms* in Solihull, when a stranger appeared and took him to one side. The stranger sported a sandy beard and moustache and wore a long Ulster coat. People who overheard their conversation agreed it was in a foreign language, probably Irish. After a while the two men were seen going into the rear yard. Suddenly a bang was heard from that direction.

The first men who rushed into the yard saw Thomas clutching his side. Nearby stood the stranger with a gun in his hand, who took one hard look at his surprised audience. No one tried to stop him as he fled. He was not to be seen again for another five years.

They took Thomas to the workhouse infirmary where he died the next day. Soon a murder enquiry had started under the control of Superintendent Joseph Yardley.

One of his tasks was to search Thomas's room, where he found documents relating to the Irish Defence Fund. Now the killing took on a new political perspective: even more so when the murderer was identified as John Duff, a young Irishman. Duff worked at Kynoch's factory in Witton and was known to have purchased some pistols recently. One was a 4.42 calibre – identical to the bullet which killed Thomas. Establishing a motive was not so easy although Yardley was convinced it was connected with the Irish question. His theories were reinforced by the discovery of code books in Duff's room. These showed details of sticks (rifles), pills (bullets) and bene (bayonets) which Duff had acquired. It seemed obvious to him that Duff had been sent to kill Thomas. The question was why? Until Duff was arrested it would have to remain unanswered.

Meanwhile Duff had disappeared without trace and remained so until 1885 when information was received to say he was working and living in London under the name of James Wallace. Inspector Hall, who knew Duff, was detailed to find him. As recognition can work both ways, Hall took great care to change his appearance and prepared for a long search of London's dock lands. His only companion was a detective from the Metropolitan Police.

Travelling through the Strand one morning, Hall saw Duff on another bus. Jumping out of his seat, he called to his colleague to follow and ran after his quarry. It was an unbelievable stroke of good luck. Leaping on the other bus the police officers pushed past the amazed conductor and arrested the fugitive.

Initially Duff denied having been in the *Gardeners Arms* that fateful Sunday. He explained how he had left the area because of the ribbing he was getting from his friends concerning his similar appearance to that published of the killer. Hall remained unimpressed. Duff tried another tale and claimed he had not been out of London. Unfortunately his seaman's papers showed him having been to sea on at least five occasions during this time using the names James Wallace.

In November 1885 Duff pleaded not guilty to murder at Warwick Assizes. By any standards it was not a good example of lawyers at work. To be fair the prosecution insisted on him being tried as an Englishman. They did not want any bias being shown against him as current feelings were running high against the Irish.

Duff then tried to turn Queen's evidence against the Irish Republican Brotherhood. He argued it was the Brotherhood who had sent him to kill Thomas. Duff explained how he was really against the idea and had never wanted to harm him. Once this offer had been rejected, he changed his defence yet again.

Now he claimed the shooting had been an accident. In support of this, a written statement from Canon O'Sullivan was produced. For some reason, the Canon was never required to testify in person for either side. He had interviewed Thomas shortly before he died and wrote down what was virtually a dying declaration. All the same, there must be a big question mark over the Canon's testimony:-

Canon	"You believe this as an accident?"
Thomas	"It might have been."
Canon	"Well you had no enemies?"
Thomas	"No."
Canon	"Then it must have been an accident?"
Thomas	"Yes."
Canon	"I believe you are connected with some political societies. Is there any reason for them to take your life?"
Thomas	"No."

There was other conversation including a suggestion that Thomas knew the identity of his killer. Yet nobody asked his name! The judge was very critical of the Canon not being called.

At last the judge summed up. He emphasised the Irish connection and how Thomas had been shot at very close range, as proved by the powder burns on his waistcoat. It was up to the jury to decide whether or not the shooting was deliberate.

For Duff it was to be a long wait. As dusk fell the jury were escorted to the *Warwick Arms Hotel* and locked up for the night. After deliberating for seven hours, they reached a verdict.

There was an astonished gasp from the spectators at their verdict of not guilty to the murder charge. Duff's relief however was short lived as they found him guilty of manslaughter instead. The judge was not impressed by the verdict and ensured Duff would spend the next 20 years in penal servitude!

18

A DEGRADING SPECTACLE

(1881 – Wishaw)

S uddenly the dreaded cry of "Police!" rang out as officers were seen approaching. In an instant the fight was abandoned and it was every man for himself. James Highland found himself bundled into a coach and driven away. His opponent, James Carney, was not so lucky. He was arrested with four of the spectators.

Highland's good fortune did not last long. Within a few days he had died and James Carney found himself charged with manslaughter.

The morning of 7 October 1881 had begun as a typical autumnal day when Carney and Highland left Birmingham in the early hours. They had hoped to keep their departure fairly quiet. But such was their following that they found themselves accompanied by a large crowd which effectively put an end to any hope of secrecy. Both men were prize-fighters and would be having a bare knuckle contest that day.

At last they arrived at their destination in Wishaw near Coleshill where a boxing ring had already been erected. Large sums of money were wagered on the result. In spite of being outlawed, prize fighting was still alive with quite a following, although it had been diminishing for some years and no longer included royalty amongst its ranks. The magistrates, aided by the police, now enjoyed increasing success in stopping such events happening. Consequently venues tended to be close to county boundaries such as Wishaw to frustrate their attempts.

It was a barbarous pastime with a variety of rules depending on the venue. The Marquis of Queensbury's noble ideas were completely ignored with heads and feet being used as well as fists. A round ended with a fall or a clinch. When contestants were evenly matched, a round could last for a few seconds or up to a quarter of an hour. No prizefighter would consider giving up until he was so battered and bruised as to be incapable of any further fight.

The fight between Highland and Carney had been arranged in the early summer but was delayed pending Carney's return from America. With both men claiming to be the lightweight champion of England, it promised to be an exciting contest which would make the winner £50 richer. Interested followers of prize fighting had a first class intelligence system advising them of forthcoming events. But so did the police.

Highland went on the offensive the moment the contest started, but Carney defended himself quite ably. Suddenly the fight turned in his favour as he broke through his opponent's guard and began to batter him severely about the face. By the time they reached the 63rd round, both men were bleeding profusely but neither showed any sign of surrender. It was at this point the police appeared.

Highland's rescuers soon realised their man had been badly mauled. To make matters worse he caught a chill which led to a severe inflammation of his lungs. Ignoring all advice he commenced a bout of heavy drinking and died soon afterwards.

Twelve days after the fight, James Hodgkins, Harry Bagnall, William Price and John Broom appeared at Coleshill magistrates Court. They were charged with being engaged in an unlawful assembly by aiding and abetting a prize fight. Carney appeared in the same court on a charge of manslaughter. The prosecution wanted him to stand trial at Warwick Assizes, and the other men at Quarter Sessions. The defence attempted to resolve the matter by having them bound over to keep the peace. But the chairman of the bench committed all five for trial at the Assizes. However, he was prepared to remand them all on bail.

Needless to say, the trial attracted a great deal of notoriety and interest. The courtroom was packed with spectators when the men appeared. Carney was to be tried first and would be the most interesting case. Much would depend on the prosecution witnesses. Highland's widow maintained she knew nothing about her husband's prize fighting activities. He had explained his injuries as having been caused whilst falling off a ginger beer cart. He was examined two days after the fight by a doctor who could not find any physical marks on him! In his opinion Highland's growing lung congestion had been caused by his chill.

The subsequent post mortem revealed the cause of death as being double pleurisy and pneumonia following a severe battering of the chest wall. The cause could not be explained. It might have been from a fall, chill or even a session of heavy drinking.

If the prosecution could not link Highland's fatal injuries to the fight, then Carney was on safer ground. A steady stream of witnesses testified to Highland's heavy drinking. Others said they had seen him fall off the ginger beer cart. However, many of these witnesses were disbelieved by the jury and Carney was found guilty and sentenced to six months imprisonment with hard labour.

The second trial now began. From the outset the prosecution alleged Harry Bagnall had been one of the seconds and not just a spectator. If so then his offence would be more serious and the charge upgraded to aid and abet manslaughter. The defence countered this argument successfully. Merely attending a prize fight, in which one of the contestants died, was not sufficient to justify a manslaughter charge. The judge agreed and the original charges stood. They were found guilty and sentenced to four months imprisonment. Unlike Carney, there was no mention made of any hard labour accompanying the sentence.

At the end of the trial, the judge commended the Chief Constable, Captain Brinkley, for his diligence in stopping the fight and bringing the participants to justice. He commented further: "It was idle on the part of those who believed or indulged in prize fights to say they were an exhibition of strength and skill or an illustration of British pluck and endurance. They were nothing of the kind and it could not be too generally recognised that they were a notorious, disgusting and degrading spectacle often accompanied with violence or drunkenness to which a stop must be put."

19

A QUESTION OF INTENT

(1882 – Leamington)

Herbert Allen's reaction was sudden and extremely violent. How dare Rose Holtom spurn his latest offer of marriage!

They had first met some years before in London where Rose was in service. Herbert was a joiner by trade and for him it was love at first sight. Their ensuing courtship was to last for the next two years. Friends described them as an ideal couple, until Herbert asked Rose to marry him. Much to his great dismay she was quite indifferent to the idea. In despair he moved to Birmingham. 1882 found Rose working as a parlour-maid for Mr Montgomery at Lillington Manor in Leamington Spa.

In spite of moving away, Herbert continued seeing Rose at Lillington Manor on a regular basis. He became so well known by Mr Montgomery's other servants, they did not hesitate to invite him into their sitting room when he called one evening in May 1882. Believing his visit could only mean trouble, Rose was reluctant to see him.

Herbert received her latest rejection in silence for a moment before losing his temper completely. Leaping up he grabbed her throat with one hand before pulling a revolver out of his pocket which he pointed at her heart. Rose reacted swiftly. Grabbing the revolver by the barrel she pushed it away screaming loudly as she did so. Suddenly the gun went off. Luckily for her the bullet missed. Undeterred Herbert forced the barrel round to point at Rose again. Just then the door was thrust open and George Ainge and William Haines burst into the room and grappled with Herbert. In spite of his struggles, they managed to disarm him. Another short struggle ensued whilst they held him pending the arrival of the police who had been summoned already by another servant. By the time Police Constable Henry Wise arrived, Herbert had calmed down. After being arrested he was taken to Leamington Police Station by carriage as he had refused to walk.

Herbert had been staying in lodgings in Upper Bedford Street, Leamington, which were searched by the police later that night. His landlady gave them Herbert's carpet bag. They took it back to the police station before opening it in Herbert's presence. Inside they found a box designed to hold fifty ball cartridges. Five were missing and Herbert's revolver only held five shots.

Next morning Herbert appeared at Leamington magistrates Court, where he was remanded in custody. The magistrates commented on how lucky he was not to be facing a charge of murder. He replied angrily, "I'm sorry it's not!" On leaving the dock he savagely attacked Henry Wise before other officers came to his rescue. Herbert was removed forcibly from the court.

His committal to Warwick Assizes for trial soon followed where he duly appeared later that month. He pleaded not guilty to charges of attempted murder and shooting with intent to cause grievous bodily harm. Meanwhile the prosecution had been busy. Although there were no secrets about Herbert and Rose's love affair, a real bonus appeared concerning an earlier attempt on Rose's life. Apparently Herbert had tried to throw her in the River Thames one evening. He was a very excitable character who had even tried to commit suicide on at least one occasion.

The prosecution barrister opened his case by emphasising how the facts spoke for themselves and could not really be contested. One by one Mr Montgomery's servants were called without any problems. then it was Mr Montgomery's turn. He testified to having gone to investigate the shot and seeing his servants holding Herbert. He added how Herbert had pointed the gun at him. This allegation was denied strenuously. The prosecution agreed Herbert was a respectable man who was clearly upset by Rose's rejection of his marriage proposals. All the evidence pointed to him being quite sober at the time.

So concluded the prosecution evidence. Now the court settled down expectantly and waited to see what case the defence would produce.

There followed a succession of witnesses all of whom testified to Herbert's previous good character. Their evidence was not contested. The sudden unexpected appearance of Rose's sister caused a murmur of anticipation in court which was silenced quickly. But her evidence on Herbert's behalf was not controversial. After the last witness the defence barrister summed up.

He could not contest what had happened. It was not a question of whether the gun went off in the struggle or if Herbert's conduct had been diabolical or violent. What mattered was whether or not he had shot at Rose intending to harm her. If murder had been on his mind, why did he not pull the trigger when he had her by the throat and completely in his power. It was a question of intent.

He knew it was a powerful argument and he had the undivided attention of everybody in the court. He pressed on whilst he had the advantage. After all, he insisted, Herbert had been waiting to marry Rose for years and could not get an answer from her. It was hardly surprising he was upset.

The judge was less impressed, being highly critical of people who carried firearms without a very good reason. He could find no justification for Herbert having such a weapon.

A good lawyer can put forward all manner of interpretations of a client's actions even when they appear simple and clear cut. Many lawyers have experienced having seen their watertight cases slowly crumbling before their eyes and juries are famous for making unexpected verdicts. This was to be the case with Herbert Allen.

After a retirement of only a few minutes, the jury returned a verdict of not guilty on both charges. The court was stunned.

The prosecution reacted quickly, determined to have the last word. Before he left the dock, Herbert was further charged with common assault. He pleaded guilty and was sentenced to nine months imprisonment with hard labour. He had remained impassive throughout the entire proceedings.

20

THE WARWICK BANKERS

(1887 – Warwick)

George Cable Lake was worried as he wrestled with his conscience. Whilst still feeling some loyalty towards his former employees, he had lost his position at the bank. Also he was totally shocked by the callous attitude shown by them to their unfortunate creditors. He did not know what to do. Should he tell the Official Receiver what he knew or just keep quiet?

In September 1887 the unthinkable had happened. The long established and highly reliable Greenway Smith and Greenway Bank in Warwick had gone into receivership. The crash caused heavy losses to many of the bank's clients. For a while they still maintained a degree of trust in the senior partners – the well respected Kelynge Greenway and his brother George who was a solicitor and Town Clerk of Warwick. This misplaced trust soon evaporated.

Once the petition for bankruptcy had been filed, George's last known honourable act was to resign from being Town Clerk. From now on it was to be a continuous running battle between the brothers and their creditors. They tried to present themselves as the innocent parties in the affair whilst openly defying their creditors. When they obtained the services of the country's leading lawyers to find ways of evading their responsibilities, the brothers made many enemies.

Their attitude aroused the suspicions of Thomas Peirson the Official Receiver and encouraged him to really scrutinise the bankers' affairs. There was no shortage of evidence of their extravagance. They both had extensive personal overdrafts at their own bank and obviously made a habit of living off their creditors. Slowly Peirson tried to piece a case together for their public examination. But he desperately needed some evidence of fraud, being convinced it had taken place.

In early 1888 farm labourer Richard Walsh was prosecuted for threatening to kill Kelynge. As Walsh had lost money when the bank failed, he was treated leniently by the magistrates. Peirson was disappointed the Walsh affair did not lead to other aggrieved creditors coming forward. By now he was coming under immense pressure to obtain maximum compensation for the creditors. It was an uphill struggle. George's house was up for sale, but Kelynge's wife had her own money which she used for her husband's benefit regardless of the misery he had caused to his many creditors. No doubt Kelynge hoped it would all blow over, but he had reckoned without George Lake the former bank manager. He had an interesting tale to tell the Official Receiver about Frederick Cooper's bill of exchange.

In the mid 1870's Frederick returned after many years in Australia and took up residence locally, becoming a client of Greenways. He received regular payments from his Australian investments by way of bills of exchange. Not wanting the responsibility of them before payment was due, he paid them into Greenways for onward transmission to Glynn's Bank in London for redeeming. Greenways would then pay the money over to Frederick.

On 15 August 1887 Frederick gave Greenways a bill of exchange value £1200 which was not ready for payment. When Greenways ceased trading the following month he demanded the bill's return. His letter was acknowledged then filed. But George Lake knew what had really happened after refusing to be involved in the transactions which were handled by Kelynge.

On 20 August Greenways owned Glynn's Bank £3943. One week later the debt had been reduced by £2812, which included the use of Frederick's £1200. Unbeknown to him, Kelynge had 'borrowed' his money. Peirson was delighted. Now he had evidence of fraud against at least one of the brothers. It encouraged him to investigate further – with interesting results.

George Greenway had used a client's money, held in trust by the bank, to purchase shares in a company where he was a director.

Later he sold shares without informing the Trust. The money he made on the deal was paid into Greenways in a futile attempt to pay off the bank's rapidly accumulating debts.

On 30 July 1888 the brothers appeared at Warwick Assizes. They were jointly charged in relation to George's purchase and sale of the shares. Kelynge was further charged in relation to Frederick's bill of exchange. They pleaded not guilty and such was the interest in the trial admittance had to be by ticket only. About 90% would-be spectators were turned away.

The start of the trial was delayed because Kelynge was standing outside the court talking to some friends. Defended by Sir Charles Russell, reputed to be the best lawyer in the land, with a retainer of 500 guineas, it was yet another example of his flamboyant style and disregard for his creditors. Sir Charles earned his money by successfully arguing on technicalities which resulted in Kelynge being acquitted of any involvement in the sale of the shares. George was not so lucky. Any relief Kelynge might have felt was quickly dashed when he was found guilty on the other charge.

The creditors had the satisfaction of seeing George Greenway sentenced to five years in prison. They were not so impressed with the judges leniency sentencing Kelynge to just 12 months in Warwick Gaol.

Early one morning a year later, the doors of Warwick Gaol opened and a pale and thinner Kelynge emerged, free at last. Having hoped for a quiet release, he found himself greeted by an angry crowd. They grabbed him, none too gently and frog marched him to Warwick railway station, where he was put on the first available train and given a single ticket. Kelynge was told, in no uncertain terms, never to return to Warwick. The crowd waited on the platform until the train moved off.

At the last minute the departure of the train was delayed to await the arrival of a police constable who was handcuffed to a prisoner. They were returning to Birmingham and boarded the waiting train. Much to the crowd's satisfaction, they entered the same compartment in which Kelynge was sitting. He was not amused.

21

SECOND OPINION
(1887 – Kineton)

Robert Rudland was both surprised and hurt when his employer refused to see him. After all, he thought, it had only been a slight scuffle the night before, not a full scale fight. Sadly he left the house hoping the other man's health and temper would improve as the day progressed. Little did he realise he would never see his employer again.

Prior to his early and unexpected death, John Garbutt Hutchinson had been a successful doctor with a rapidly expanding country practice and a promising future. The pressure of work had necessitated him employing an assistant – Robert Rudland. Yet, everything was not quite as rosy as it appeared. In spite of the numerous pleas from his very young wife, John Hutchinson was a heavy drinker.

A familiar figure, Hutchinson spent most nights drinking locally with numerous companions. Usually his last call was at the *Kineton Village Club* with his assistant. The club was well known for serving alcohol at all hours of the day or night and Hutchinson took advantage of its reputation. The night of 3 October 1887 had been no exception.

Sometime after midnight the two men left the club and made their unsteady way home. They were in high spirits and normally comfortable in each others company. But this night was different. Crossing the churchyard they began to argue. Inflamed by alcohol the argument became heated and they ended up fighting.

The cause of the fracas remains unknown, but Rudland was adamant it was more of a scuffle than a fight. Nevertheless he managed to black his employer's eye. The scuffle sobered them and Rudland took the other man back home leaving him in the care of his wife. Thinking the matter would blow over during the night he was dismayed to find Hutchinson unwell later that morning. He was even more upset to find himself prevented from entering his employer's house and speaking to him. Even his offer to medically treat the man's ailments was refused. Hutchinson had shut himself away drinking and not allowing anybody near him.

In the following days his condition worsened and finally he agreed to seek medical advice from Symes McVicar, a doctor from nearby Shennington. After the first visit McVicar moved into his patient's house. However, his treatment appeared to be having no effect and Rudland suggested to ought to obtain a second opinion.

McVicar refused. Confident in his own ability and experience, he considered Rudland to be unqualified and totally scorned any of his suggestions. At the same time he ensured Rudland was not allowed anywhere near his stricken employer. Five days later Hutchinson died.

When the inquest opened at the *Red Lion* in Kineton, nobody foresaw its eventual outcome. It soon became the centre of attraction for miles around with many spectators. Also present was police Superintendent George Hinde. Suspicious by nature he knew about the earlier fight and had many questions to ask. Rudland was the first witness.

In most people's eyes he was the real villain of the affair. Whilst he admitted giving Hutchinson an occasional mixture of bromide of potash to stop him drinking, he denied strenuously using it as a tonic. The spectators were clearly disappointed when he was allowed to leave the witness stand. However, McVicar's testimony quickly re-aroused their interest.

It started straightforwardly with his being called to the house where he found Hutchinson very drunk and suffering from delirium tremors. Suddenly McVicar's answers became very evasive especially concerning the way he had treated his patient. Initially admitting using bromide of potash and cholal, he now confessed to using laudanum. His confidence returned briefly when he agreed he had relied on his own experience, dismissing any idea of a second opinion, especially from Rudland. Confusion returned quickly as his cross-examination proceeded. Soon it became quite clear he was a heavy drinker also and had been drunk for most of the time.

George Hinde continued relentlessly. McVicar became even more confused, being unable to remember what treatment he had prescribed or even where he had slept! Finally the coroner adjourned the inquest and ordered a post-mortem examination to be carried out on Hutchinson's body.

It resumed the next day with McVicar still representing himself without any legal assistance. The post-mortem revealed the intemperance of Hutchinson's internal organs but nothing else. The coroner remained concerned about the possibility the deceased might have been poisoned and insisted the stomach contents were sent to Birmingham for a detailed analysis. The inquest was adjourned again.

Thankfully McVicar left the *Red Lion* only to find his path blocked by George Hinde and several police officers. Worse followed as he was arrested and taken to Warwick Gaol.

When the inquest resumed, McVicar remained in gaol, however, he was ably represented by Mr Crowther-Davies. Initially his criticisms of the police went unheeded until the analyst confirmed no trace of any poison had been found in the deceased's stomach. With his mind at rest on the poison issue, the coroner agreed with Crowther-Davies. McVicar could not deny being hopelessly drunk when treating his patient. But, argued Crowther-Davies, the all important question was whether or not he was sober when he actually made up the prescriptions. Finally he dismissed any idea of Rudland being sufficiently qualified to offer a second opinion.

The jury's verdict was 'death by misadventure' and they strongly criticised McVicar's drunken conduct during the treatment of his patient. Even then George Hinde refused to cede defeat. Two days later McVicar found himself before the Kineton magistrates charged with Hutchinson's manslaughter.

Once again he was defended by Crowther-Davies. McVicar's excited and confused state at the inquest was blamed on the stress the affair had caused him. It was a compelling argument. By now George Hinde recognised defeat. During a short adjournment he consulted with the chief constable and all the charges were dropped.

Although McVicar left the court a free man, his reputation was in tatters. His obstinate refusal to seek a second opinion had cost him dear.

22

RAT'S REVENGE

(1889 – Leamington)

D r William Horniblow stared at the crystals he had just discovered in the rat's cage. They looked like corrosive sublimate to him. If so, he thought, that would explain the sudden death of his wife's pet rat a few days earlier. But how had they got into the cage, he wondered. Suddenly recent events in the household became clear.

Earlier in February 1889 his wife, Elizabeth, had suffered a sudden paralysis. Unable to nurse her and tend his house, practice and fourteen year old son William, he had employed Sarah Kibler as housekeeper. Sarah quickly took over the running of the house and surgery in Clarendon Terrace, Leamington Spa. Within the month father and son were relieved to see Elizabeth begin to recover. Unfortunately Sarah did not share their happiness. She had other plans to remain as housekeeper with all the material benefits such a position included. Consequently any improvement in Elizabeth's health was the last thing she wanted. So she began to explore other more drastic ways to ensure her current employment remained permanent.

Being responsible for cleaning the surgery Sarah had a good idea about what was stored there. She decided to use corrosive sublimate which she knew to be very poisonous. Before administering the poison, she began spreading rumours about Elizabeth's illness being so serious that there was little chance of her surviving. By 7 March she was ready for the next stage of her plan.

That afternoon Elizabeth asked Sarah to make her a cup of tea. Sarah did so and took the opportunity of adding some corrosive sublimate to the brew. With a thumping heart she handed the tea to her mistress and watched her swallow the first mouthful. The reaction was spectacular.

Elizabeth spat it out immediately complaining about it tasting of copper and sulphur. Then she was violently sick which probably saved her life. Several days later Elizabeth still complained about her mouth and throat burning. As the symptoms passed the incident was forgotten.

About a week later, Sarah made a point of speaking to Joseph Bellamy the milkman. She told him Elizabeth could never recover. Then she embellished the story by telling him a man's footstep had been heard on the landing. Gravely she explained this was a sign of impending death. Joseph liked the Horniblows and went away sadly convinced Elizabeth was dying. It is easy to imagine his surprise some days later when he saw her walking and not looking anything like near death. However, four days later there was a death in the Horniblow house.

It was Elizabeth's pet rat. The animal had died quite unnaturally with a very swollen body. Sarah was delighted. Firstly because she detested the creature but more importantly the experiment had worked. All she needed was something to disguise the taste of the poison. Meanwhile, Elizabeth was too upset to clear away the cage and it was left for the time being.

Elizabeth's health continued improving and Sarah realised her days in Clarendon Terrace were numbered. She would have to act soon or it would be too late. Her chance came one afternoon when she saw Elizabeth mix herself a brandy and water. Before tasting it, she went into the garden with her son leaving the drink unattended on the table. Quickly Sarah put the poison into it and waited impatiently for her mistress to drink it. At last Elizabeth returned and took a sip.

She spat it out at once complaining of the taste and threw the cup down on the table where it broke. Quickly removing the broken cup and tablecloth, Sarah knew she had failed. Her employment ended in early April when she left the household. Deep down she knew she was lucky not to have been discovered. She had long since forgotten about the rat, but unbeknown to her, that poor creature was about to have its revenge.

At last Elizabeth felt strong enough to dispose of the rat's cage. Unable to face doing it herself her husband was to do it for her. It was when he removed the rat's little rug, to give to Elizabeth as a memento, that he saw the crystals. He called the family together and they remembered it was Sarah who had been responsible for looking after the rat during Elizabeth's illness. Any lingering doubts any of them had were quickly dispelled when the broken cup was recovered from the dustbin. More crystals of corrosive sublimate could be seen.

Intent on prosecuting Sarah, Dr Horniblow approached the magistrates. However, they declined to accept his information, allegedly because it was not sworn on the Bible as he had insisted on affirming. Annoyed but undeterred, he commenced his own investigation. An analysis of the suspect crystals confirmed they were corrosive sublimate. A confrontation between the two women was not so productive. It ended with William referring to Sarah as 'a...... old hag!' (His actual words are not recorded). Armed with this new evidence William found the magistrates prepared to listen to him. In late December Sarah appeared at Warwick Assizes where she pleaded not guilty to attempted murder.

Although the judge described the trial as 'a serious case', it was not without its humourous moments. In particular Mr Hugo Young, acting for Sarah, continually referred to Dr Horniblow as Hornblower, and to be corrected on each occasion amid much laughter. The Birmingham City analyst described finding thirty grains of corrosive sublimate in the brandy cup. As just three grains would cause death Elizabeth had been very lucky.

After a retirement of just fifteen minutes the jury found Sarah guilty. She continued protesting her innocence as the judge sentenced her to fifteen years penal servitude. As Sarah was led away she turned to Dr Horniblow and warned him darkly how he would 'have to answer on his death bed.' Before hearing the next case, the judge soundly criticised the Leamington magistrates for failing to act on William's first complaint.

23

THE ALIBI

(1891 – Warwick)

Only a few yards from the barracks Sarah Carty stopped worrying about the strange man who had been following her. It was a bad mistake. Suddenly he ran up and grabbed her with one hand whilst waving a golf marker threateningly with his other. "Stand still!" he snarled. "Move if you dare!"

Earlier Sarah had left her home in Stand Street, Warwick to walk across the common to the nearby Budbrooke Barracks, home of the Royal Warwickshire Regiment. It was a warm, light and pleasant evening on 8 May 1891. She had made the journey, which normally took her about 25 minutes, many times. Her husband Timothy was a retired Colour Sergeant in the Regiment, and their son, Richard, currently stationed at the barracks, now held the same rank.

To supplement their income Sarah laundered various items of linen for the officers mess. On this particular evening she was returning a parcel of thirty four napkins to the barracks. As usual she walked across the common, over the Gog Brook and into the nearby fields. It was when she crossed the brook she first noticed the stranger following her and assumed he was heading for the barracks. However, she was somewhat disconcerted to see he was carrying an iron golf marker, complete with flag, in one hand.

Sarah continued her journey passing Corporals Shepherd and Woodward walking towards Warwick. The stranger still followed her. About thirty yards from the barracks she saw Sergeant Colgan's wife standing in a window and the women waved to each other. Then the stranger struck.

Taking one look at him brandishing the golf marker Sarah

screamed "Murder!" In reply he swung the marker hitting her hard on the head. Sarah fell to her knees and dropped the bundle of linen. Undeterred by the shouts from the barracks and the running soldiers, the stranger dropped the marker and knelt beside the moaning woman. Quickly he seized her purse and the linen before running off towards Hatton, swiftly pursued by several soldiers. As he ran, he ripped open her bundle. Finding it full of linen napkins he thew it down in disgust and continued leaving his pursuers behind.

Meanwhile Sergeant Colgan had rushed out to Sarah. He found she had lost a fair amount of blood. When Richard Carty reached his mother he was torn between staying with her and joining in the hunt for the attacker. In all the confusion the man escaped.

As several of the sergeants had their own bicycles they quickly organised themselves into a posse and set off towards the Hatton and Birmingham direction. Just outside Knowle they came across a man who fitted the description of Sarah's attacker. As can well be imagined they took him into custody none too gently. Unfortunately he was not the culprit and had to be released.

Somewhat dejectedly they returned to Warwick to find the police had been and gone, but the culprit still remained free. The good news was Sarah's wounds were not too serious and it was hoped she would make a full recovery.

About one and a half hours after the robbery, Police Constable James Sloss was walking home to Kenilworth after having been on duty at Warwick. Somewhere near Gaveston by Leek Wooton Spinney, he overtook 44 year old Edward Bowring, an itinerant labourer. An army pensioner, Bowring was described as being of a 'scruffy tramp like appearance'. Bowring called out to the Constable and they walked together for a while. Later James would recall Bowring had been acting quite normally.

After parting company James went home and thought no more about the encounter. He was reminded of it quite abruptly the next day when he read about the attack on Sarah. Having seen the description, he was in no doubt it was the man who had walked with him that night. More to the point, he remembered where the man had been heading. Later that day he went to Leicester and helped arrest Bowring. He was surprised to see the prisoner was wearing different clothes from the day before.

Throughout the journey back to Warwick Bowring protested his innocence, and denied knowing where the barracks were situated. But his protestations fell on deaf ears and on 1 August 1891 Bowring stood in the dock at Warwick Assizes. He pleaded not guilty, steadfastly maintaining he had been elsewhere at the time of the attack.

Sarah was the first witness. She related the events of the night of the robbery and agreed she had identified Bowring in gaol. Other witnesses followed who had identified the prisoner whilst he was in gaol. Each remarked how Bowring was wearing different clothes on the evening of the attack. Their accounts were corroborated by PC Sloss before Bowring gave his evidence.

He continued saying he had been elsewhere at the time of the crime and set out to prove it. His first witness was David Palethorpe. who related having met Bowring in the Coventry Road and gave him a penny. Whilst Bowring was adamant they had parted at about 7.00 p.m., Palethorpe insisted the time was nearer 6.30 p.m. adding he last saw Bowring heading back towards Warwick. What is unclear is whereabouts in the Coventry Road they actually met.

James Mumford was the next witness. He had drunk with Bowring in the *New Bowling Green* at about 8.00 p.m. There was an expectant hush as Rose Pettipher took the stand. She was a barmaid in the *New Bowling Green* and her evidence would be crucial. Rose agreed she had been on duty the night of the attack, but could not recall having seen Bowring at the inn. With his defence collapsing around him, Bowring's lawyer had little else to offer. Although he tried hard, no evidence could be produced to give any credence to Bowring's alibi. The jury were not sympathetic and the defendant was found guilty. Equally the judge was not very sympathetic. Bowring found himself sentenced to 18 months imprisonment with hard labour.

24

IT OUGHT TO HAVE BEEN DONE YEARS AGO

(1892 – Leamington)

Turning into Guys Cliffe Road, James Greatrex was surprised to see his wayward son William standing there. From his stance it was clear this was no accidental meeting. Vividly he recalled the last letter from his son in which William had threatened to kill him.

Icy fear clutched at the old man's heart as he saw the revolver in William's hand. From bitter experience James knew it was pointless trying to reason with his son. There was only one chance and he started to run. Coolly William raised his revolver and fired.

Seventy-four years old James had retired from his successful saddlery business in Walsall some years previously and had moved to Leamington. Apart from the death of his wife a few weeks earlier, the only problem was William, who was unemployed and relied entirely on the allowance paid to him by James. But it was not enough to support his extravagant life style of living in London.

Over the years James had financed numerous business ventures for his son, mainly in America and Australia. But they had all failed and a disgruntled William returned to London. During the course of his mother's funeral, William had tried to obtain yet more money from James, who had refused and they had parted angrily. Afterwards William had written and threatened his father. William was used to threatening people. Among his other victims was his landlady in London whom he had promised to kill along with her bantam cocks.

On the morning of 31 May 1892 James went for his usual morning walk with his sister-in-law Rebecca Ryder. His route never varied. It was then he was confronted by his son.

William first shot hit the old man in the back. He staggered a few yards before collapsing on the pavement. Rebecca watched helplessly as William stood over his father and fired again. This time James was hit in the heart. As the sound of the shot died away, William felt his arm being pulled. He found himself being held by Thomas Hubbard who had witnessed the whole event from the nearby *Coventry Arms* public house. William did not move. Even he seemed stunned by what had happened. Moments later Constable George Crowther ran out of Heath Terrace. Calmly William surrendered his revolver to him saying, "I have got him with the second shot. It ought to have been done years ago."

As William was taken away, James was carried into a nearby house. Dr Thursfield arrived quickly after being summoned. Realising there was a bullet in the old man's heart, he knew it was too late. James was carried back to his home in Moss Close.

William was taken to Leamington Police Station where he was searched. He was found to be in possession of a large sum of money and some prussic acid. He remained emotionless throughout and only became excited when asked questions about the actual shooting. He never expressed any regrets about having murdered his father. Later he admitted having intended to shoot himself. He had not expected to use two bullets in James and that had disrupted his plans.

From the outset the case aroused a great deal of interest. Consequently it was not surprising the magistrates court was full to overflowing when William made his first appearance the next day. He entered the court with a jaunty air and listened to the evidence against him. Constable Crowther testified to having made the arrest and later searching his lodgings in Warwick. Here he found wine, £20, clothing and more bullets for William's gun. As expected William was remanded in custody for a week. On leaving the dock he was hissed and booed by the spectators.

Two days later an inquest was held on the body of James Greatrex. Dr Thursfield described how the revolver had been fired at very close quarters. Nobody was surprised when the verdict of wilful murder was given. James was buried later that day.

When William next appeared in court, it was just as crowded. Just before being committed for trial he addressed the court. "No one knows the treatment I have received from my father. I ought to have done it in 1884 and I have been in America for five years. I had fever and dysentery and was very ill." If William had expected any sympathy he was to be sadly disappointed. His outburst was greeted by renewed boos and hisses from the spectators. At the end of July William stood trial at Warwick Assizes where he pleaded not guilty.

Everything centred around the allowances James had paid to his son. Over the years these had increased usually following threats from William. The previous year his annual allowance had been raised to £350 provided the threats stopped. For a while all was well, but then the threats started again. By now James had made up his mind. He would not give into any more of his son's threats.

The only chance the defence had was on the question of William's sanity. It was a difficult task made even harder when the medical witnesses disagreed. After an absence of only sixteen minutes the jury returned a verdict of guilty. However, they added a rider that he was not responsible for his actions and thereby saved his life. William was sentence to imprisonment for an indefinite period.

The tragedy was made even more poignant by the inscription inside William's watch which was found by the police during their enquiries;

> "To William Ernest Greatrex on his coming of age
> October 23rd 1873 by his affectionate father".

Then came the real sting in the tail. When the murdered man's will was published, William was due to inherit £8000! Needless to say the family was scandalised and opposed the bequest through the court. Common sense prevailed when the court agreed with the family. It would have been improper for a murderer to gain any financial benefit from his crime. William was prevented from. receiving the money.

25

A CRUEL WOMAN

(1892 – Warton)

Throughout that short summer night in 1892 Rachel Slate cowered in her employer's garden. When dawn finally came she left her shelter and went into Warton village. In spite of having no clear idea where she was going, Rachel thought anywhere was preferable to the cruelty being left behind.

Having been in service before, Rachel had willingly accepted the position offered her by Marion Humphris's father; working at Warton for £9 per annum plus her food and lodging. Whatever her hopes and expectations might have been, she was quickly disillusioned.

For a short while everything went well, until Marion began complaining the work was not being done properly and accusing her of being lazy. Single handed Rachel had a ten roomed house to clean as well as care for Marion and her family. She rarely got to bed before 3.00 a.m., only to be called two to three hours later. But that was only the beginning of her trouble.

In spite of the promises made about food, there were no regular meals for her. Occasionally there might be, but mostly she was lucky if she was given anything at all to eat. Towards the end of April 1892, Marion accused her of not doing her work properly and struck the poor girl with a silver topped stick as 'thick as a thumb'. Within the month Rachel was in trouble again. This time Marion ordered her upstairs where she forced Rachel to undress and lie naked on the bed. Then she laid about the frightened girl with the stick. A week later Rachel was ordered upstairs again. At first she refused, but Marion threatened to make matters worse if she did so. Powerless to resist, Rachel allowed herself to be beaten once more.

On 7 June Rachel was subjected to another beating because the water was not hot enough for the baby's bath. Marion hit her about the face and breasts before giving her a slice of dry toast to eat. The next day there was no food at all and the provisions were locked away. In the evening she was beaten again and threatened with another. Totally exhausted both physically and mentally, she decided to run away. Waiting until Marion and her husband were eating their supper, Rachel slipped outside and hid in the garden.

On leaving the garden she had no idea where to go. Marion had only let her out of the house twice before and then only to go to church. Then Rachel's luck changed when she met Emma Stuffins. Quickly realising the girl was in great distress, Emma took her by the hand and went straight to Police Constable Harby Ford's house. In her husband's absence, Mrs Ford took charge and gave Rachel some food, but she could not keep it down. When Harby returned he described the girl as 'depressed and ill'. On seeing her discoloured shoulders it was obvious she had been treated badly.

The following month found Marion in the dock at Warwick Quarter Sessions charged with unlawfully assaulting Rachel. There was great interest in the case coming when the Nation Society for Prevention of Cruelty to Children was in its infancy. In fact its formation was blamed by some for this case being brought to court. Nobody was surprised when Marion pleaded not guilty.

Marion was reported as being dressed in a short pale green costume, black jacket and bonnet with grey feathers which 'well suited her 45 years'. Plainly her intention was to make an impression in the dock, maintaining a complete air of indignation throughout the trial. The prosecution countered by carefully pointing out that the facts were what mattered most and not the social standing of the defendant.

In a quiet, subdued manner Rachel outlined her experiences, adding she had never been paid. On complaining to Mr Humphris, he had replied it was none of his business. He denied having heard her screams, but was present on one occasion when she was being beaten. Rachel stood her ground during cross-examination especially when it was suggested how Marion had been ill since Easter with a heart complaint.

"She could still use the stick well enough!" Rachel replied spiritedly. Her reply caused a burst of laughter in court.

Dr William Smart testified to examining Rachel on behalf of the police. He described the bruises he had found on her buttocks, arms, shoulders, left breast and eyebrow. It was his opinion, shared by Constable Ford, that she had been severely beaten. The defence disagreed and produced written evidence from Dr de Caux. He alleged the marks on Rachel's body were not bruises but a result of the arsenic treatment used on her eczema. His views were ridiculed by the prosecution.

Marion's father told how he had dressed Rachel at his own expense and paid her travel expenses. The court was not impressed collapsing with laughter as he described Marion's kindness. He considered her to be totally incapable of striking a horse or dog let alone a servant girl! His views were supported by Marion's father-in-law and other employees.

In summing up, the defence concentrated on the eczema treatment. It ended by reinforcing Marion's standing in society. The judge thought Rachel might have been lazy but added it was possible she could not do the work in the time permitted. In any case, he found it hard to see what grounds could excuse such a beating.

After hearing several hours of evidence, the jury made a token retirement of five minutes before finding Marion guilty. At this point Dr de Caux was actually produced to discuss Marion's health. He agreed she was in a weak state, but could find no evidence of her alleged heart trouble.

Protesting to the end, Marion was sentenced to the very apt punishment of three months in prison with hard labour. Her father cried, "Oh! Monstrous! Monstrous!" as she was sentenced.

What made Marion's crime all the more scandalous was her position in society. She was the wife of the Vicar of Warton.

26

AN EMBARRASSING CASE

(1892 – Warwick)

P rivate Russell Bray stood still, listening. He heard the distant sound of somebody groaning again. Peering in the general direction of the sound, he could see nothing through the torrential rain. It would be easy just to walk away, but his conscience got the better of him.

Minutes later he stood in nearby Warwick Police Station telling Sergeant Webb what he had heard. Webb followed the soldier to Priory Road, where some distance away from the nearest streetlight they found a man's body. They carried him back to the police station where he died soon afterwards.

At first glance, Webb had thought the man was drunk. He soon changed his mind when he saw the injuries to his head. Clearly he had been subjected to a severe beating and the police realised they had a murder enquiry on their hands. It was just what they needed to finish off what had been 'one of those nights'.

It has started peacefully enough during that November afternoon in 1892 with the Army winning a football match against a local side at Emscote. The ensuing celebration just became an excuse for drinking and fighting all over the town for the next few hours.

When it was discovered the dead man's injuries could have been caused by belt buckles, Inspector Stephen Hall assumed the culprits were soldiers. It was common knowledge how soldiers often used their belts as weapons. Suspicion soon fell on Privates James Welch, a powerful former boxer from Birmingham, and Frederick Thomas King, a slightly built man. Hall immediately visited the barracks at nearby Budbrooke and arrested the two men. Although confined to barracks, King had in fact climbed over the wall and gone into town. On his return he was seen wearing a wet muddy greatgoat. Hall was confident he had his men, but there was very little evidence. Even the dead man was still unidentified.

The murder scene was searched thoroughly in daylight. Hall must have been relieved when a military cane, silver ring and greatcoat button were found. Looking close at King's greatcoat, he saw it appeared to be bloodstained, and the second button had been replaced with white thread. Whilst the coat was wet, the new thread was dry!

When the soldiers appeared before the magistrates the next day, a vast crowd, mainly women had gathered outside the court house. After a short hearing they were remanded in custody for a week while Hall made more enquiries. The case seemed to be going his way and he was confident of a successful outcome.

Before the week was out, the dead man was identified as 32 year old James Russell, a quiet inoffensive man with seven children who lived in the Saltisford. He was buried in Warwick Cemetery. His coffin was carried by six pall bearers from the Avon Rovers Football Club and there were many wreaths. Meanwhile Hall believed he had discovered exactly what had happened.

After the match, Welch and King had been drinking in the *Lord Nelson* where James Russell's sister Edith worked as a barmaid. The tavern was packed with soldiers and townsfolk. It was all amicable until an unidentified soldier made abusive remarks about Edith. James immediately sprung to her defence and an argument started with James being invited to 'go outside' by the soldier. He refused the 'invitation' and moved on to the *Avon Tavern*. He left there about 10.00 p.m. to make his way home and was never seen alive again. What actually happened to him is largely conjecture based on what witnesses saw or thought they saw.

Witnesses saw a man being confronted by two soldiers in Priory Road. They frog marched him away continually hitting him with their belts. Hall was adamant they were the victim and his two assailants, but the witnesses could not positively identify the men. Try as he might, no witnesses were found who could put James, King and

Welch together anywhere in Warwick that night. Gradually he became less confident in the outcome of his investigation.

He had King's greatcoat, but it was only circumstantial evidence. A hundred years later forensic science could have checked it for the dead man's blood. The silver ring was of a common variety often purchased by soldiers. To make matters worse, the button was not a Warwickshire Regimental one. All he could prove was King and Welsh's admissions to having fought during the evening with their belts. Edith Russell even denied being aware of any argument involving her brother. She had not heard anybody challenge him although he had been clearly upset about something.

In a packed courthouse the soldiers were committed for trial at the next Assizes. The Warwick Advertiser was quite graphic about the steamed up windows in the court which were described as being like 'an exotic conservatory less its purity and pleasantness of odour!'

Before actually going to trial, the case was considered by the Grand Jury. They recognised the shortcomings of the prosecution evidence which could not prove its case beyond all reasonable doubt. Consequently they had little alternative but to discontinue the proceedings. Welsh and King were discharged without ever standing trial. But the story does not end there.

Six years previously Police Constable William Hine had been savagely murdered in Fenny Compton. A few days after Welch and King's discharge, a rumour started up which linked James with PC Hine's murder. The rumour alleged James knew the identity of PC Hine's murderer. In his turn James had been murdered to ensure his silence. After having been killed, the scene was made to look like soldiers had been responsible with suitable clues left at the scene. Sadly these were just rumours and both murders remain undetected to this day.

It is always embarrassing for the police to lose a murder case. But this case was made even more to by the location of the scene of the crime. It was only a few yards from the County Police Headquarters.

27

THE ASTON AXEMAN

(1893 – Aston)

A rabella Clifford looked up at the window and her blood ran cold. Powerless to act she gazed in horror at the two silhouettes showing on the blind. Giving a long heart rending scream she ran into the house, praying she would be in time.

The story really began some six months earlier in March 1893 when her daughter, Florence, worked at Kynoch's Arms Factory in Witton, Birmingham where she met William Haynes, usually known as Billy. For Florence it was love at first sight. Although described as being little more than a child, she soon moved into rooms with him and his mother, Sarah, in William Street, Aston. For a few all too short weeks Florence was immensely happy. Tragically she did not know the truth about Billy.

Since the age of 13 he had been in continual trouble with the law. During his life of crime, Billy had been married, separated and had cohabited with two other women. Florence never knew this part of his life. Sadly Billy soon reverted to his old violent ways. He took to beating Florence regularly although she was pregnant. By mid September, she could take no more and she went home to her mother.

A quick look at her daughter's beaten face told Arabella all she needed to know. Strong willed she took hold of Florence and together they went to tackle Billy who denied the allegations. Arabella detested him and made no secret of the fact. The feeling was entirely mutual. She was adamant there would be a permanent separation. Reluctantly Florence agreed. By the following evening, arrangements had been made for Florence to collect her clothes from Billy's lodgings. Arabella accompanied her but Billy would never let her enter his rooms. Sarah took Florence into her son whilst Arabella waited anxiously outside.

Florence was alone with William and soon realised he was very drunk. Sarah had known he was drunk but relied on Florence's calming influence to keep him under control. She felt fairly confident in leaving them together. Sadly neither women had bargained on Billy's temper. As Florence gathered her few belongings, he went in to the living room. By the fire he found the axe his mother used to break up coal and wood. Gripping it tightly, Billy returned to his room and crept up behind Florence. Raising the axe over his shoulder he brought it down with sickening force on the young girl's unprotected head.

It was at this moment that Arabella looked up and saw his silhouette on the window blind.

Desperate to save her daughter's life, she ran inside and up the stairs to Billy's room. Bursting in she pleaded with him to stop. But even as she begged, he struck the defenceless girl again. Then with an evil glint in his eyes he turned on her. Before the distraught woman realised what had happened, William had struck her with the axe. Fearing now for her own life, Arabella fled downstairs to the comparative safety of the street, screaming "Murder!" as loudly as she could.

In the nearby *Sand Hill Tavern*, Thomas Hopkins was the first to react to her screams. Putting down his beer he went out to investigate, followed closely by the other customers. At Billy's lodgings, they stopped and looked at the angry man facing them with a bloodstained axe in his hands.

"Where is she?" shouted Billy. "I will kill the ......!" Suddenly he threw down the axe and walked calmly away.

Only when Thomas was certain Billy had gone, did he enter the house. Upstairs he found a badly battered Florence lying in a pool of blood. A fox terrier stood over her, licking blood off her face. To his horror, Thomas heard footsteps on the stairs, nervously he hung back waiting, uncertain of what to do. He was greatly relieved to discover the footsteps belonged to Police Constable Stephen Smythe who quickly took charge.

Florence was still alive when she was removed to the Birmingham

General Hospital where she died a few days later. Surgeon Leonard Gamgee testified later to finding four wounds in her head which had been caused by great force. The cause of death being inflammation of the brain.

On 4 October Billy walked calmly into Northampton Police Station and surrendered. Back in Aston he was questioned by Detective Sergeant Edward Cusask. He replied, "It's no use saying anything. I done it!" He blamed Arabella's interference as being the real cause of the murder.

Billy's trial at Warwick Assizes was really a formality although it lasted four and a half days. Pleading not guilty he remained impassive throughout. He had no defence and knew it. After the summing up had finished, the jury did not bother to retire, and took less than two minutes to find him guilty. It was a popular verdict. As the judge pronounced the death sentence, it was too much for Billy. "I wish I had chopped her mother" he shouted, interrupting the judge. "I would have chopped her into mincemeat. I would have made sausages of her!"

Total uproar followed which took several minutes to subside. Only when silence had resumed did the judge finish his sentencing. When it was over, Billy was led back to his cell. During this period he confessed to having stabbed a woman for which a man named Butler had been wrongly convicted. There his generosity ended as he would not make his confession on oath, and so the unfortunate Butler remained in prison.

On the morning of 2 January 1894 Billy took his last short walk on the canal side of Warwick Gaol to the execution shed. Apart from being escorted there were no elaborate preparations, just a noose attached to a single heavy beam.

Defiant to the last he called out to the assembled witnesses, "They ain't give me nuthin to eat. No breakfast nor nuthin." With reporters amongst the official witnesses his remarks were reported and denied by the Governor.

Moments later the Aston Axeman was dead. Before he died, Billy gave a souvenir matchbox to PC William Drakeley who later became Deputy Chief Constable.

28
THE ASTON ABORTIONIST

(1895 – Aston)

With Dr Fairley's fateful words still ringing in her ears, Rebecca Simister fled from his surgery.

A delicate woman, in her early 30's, Rebecca lived with her shoemaker husband and growing family in High Street, Aston in 1895. Times were hard enough without having yet another mouth to feed – and Dr Fairley had just confirmed her worst fears. She was pregnant again. Now she knew there was no alternative.

Soon afterwards, Rebecca slipped unnoticed out of her house and went to see Sarah Ann Eden. A midwife by occupation, Sarah had helped Rebecca before. Only now, it was Sarah's other services as an abortionist that Rebecca wanted.

Some two hours later, Rebecca returned home looking upset and went straight to bed. She never left it again. Not wanting Dr Fairley to visit, knowing he would suspect what had happened, she insisted on seeing Sarah who would not come until the next day. One look was enough to confirm her worst fears. Rebecca was dangerously ill and needed proper medical attention which she could not give. She sent for Dr Fairley.

He came quickly but Rebecca failed to respond to treatment and died a few days later. The cause of death was blood poisoning following the use of a sharp instrument. His suspicions were realised when Sarah confessed to him what she had done. Dr Fairley listened to her story before going to the police. Enquiries were taken over by Detective Inspector James Ravenhall. Soon information concerning another death came to light.

Later that year Sarah stood trial at Warwick Assizes and pleaded not guilty to two charges of murder. It was agreed there should be two trials. The first concerned Rebecca's death. Whilst the prosecution evidence was mainly circumstantial, the jury only took 17 minutes to find her guilty and Sarah was sentenced to death. In the ensuing uproar she collapsed and was carried out of court.

Once order was restored, Mathilda Manning entered the dock to be tried alone. The judge decreed nothing would be achieved by trying Sarah again. Mathilda's barrister successfully argued for the charge against her to be reduced to one of manslaughter.

Mathilda's story began at the Albion Hotel in Leeds where Mabel Green worked as a barmaid. One of the Albion's guests was John Hondson a commercial traveller and womaniser. Falling under his spell Mabel became pregnant. What happened next is a little unclear, but Mabel found herself in Aston living with Mathilda who was described as an old friend of Hondson.

To explain her disappearance from the Albion, Hondson arranged for a letter to be written supposedly from Mabel's mother in Aberdeen. The letter explained she was ill and needed her daughter home for a while.

Giving his evidence, Hondson clearly revelled in being the centre of attraction. He played to the spectators, continually answering glibly and smirking. He seemed incapable of seeing the danger he was in. Yes, he had been surprised to see her back in Leeds so soon especially looking so ill. Her sudden death had upset him.

Suddenly the judge interrupted and asked why he had arranged for Mabel to go to Aston. "For her confinement" came the glib reply. "After only five months?" questioned the judge, incredulously.

Any reply Hondson might have made was lost in the ensuing laughter, but the judge was not amused. Once order had been restored, he turned his full attention to Hondson warning him not to incriminate himself, before turning to the jury. He informed them Hondson was a married man with children. Finally he added, darkly, that Hondson knew far more than he was telling.

Before the judge could say any more, the foreman of the jury had a fit and collapsed. The trial was interrupted yet again whilst he was carried from the court. Hondson remained in the witness box. Addressing Mathilda, the judge told her he was satisfied she had taken Mabel to see Sarah and promptly discharged her! Scarcely able to believe her good fortune, she stumbled from the dock a free woman.

The judge's next move was to summon Inspector Ravenhall. His instructions to the police officer were quite concise. He was to arrest Hondson and to carry out a thorough investigation into his part in the whole affair.

March 1896 saw a much chastened Hondson appearing again at Warwick Assizes. This time he stood in the dock. The trial became even more appealing to the populace when word got out that 'the notorious Mrs Eden' would be called as a witness. Her death sentence had been commuted to imprisonment.

The prosecution showed Hondson to be the father of Mabel's child. Once he knew about the pregnancy, he arranged with Isabella Pirie to write pretending to be Mabel's mother. Mabel was explained as being his sister. Poor Isabella was completely duped by Hondson. Kept in ignorance of his wife and family, she had accepted his proposal of marriage. Even in gaol he had kept up the pretence of their engagement, urging her to burn his earlier letters asking her to impersonate Mabel's mother.

A stilled hush announced Sarah entering the witness box looking haggard. Surprisingly dressed in her own clothes, her address was given by Aylesbury Prison. She confirmed discussing Mathilda's pregnancy and being asked to examine a friend also.

Dr Green from Leeds stated how Mabel had died from blood poisoning, but added it could have resulted from a natural miscarriage. He believed it was not Mabel's first pregnancy.

Hondson's barrister made an impassioned plea to the effect no case had been made out by the prosecution. The judge disagreed insisting the facts were deliberated by the jury. Fifteen minutes later, just two minutes short of Sarah's verdict, they pronounced him guilty adding they felt sorry for him. The judge had no such feelings. Without waiting to don his black cap, he sentenced the prisoner to death. An unearthly quiet followed as Hondson was taken away in a state of shock.

Later his sentence was commuted to imprisonment.

29
THE TYSOE LETTERS
(1899 – Tysoe)

Dressmaker Prudence Hancox stared in total disbelief at the paper in her hand. It was a summons for her to appear at court on 30 May 1900, charged with using indecent language to the Reverend Francis Dodson, Vicar of Tysoe.

Absolutely furious, Prudence rushed out and hurried to the vicarage. She would show him! On finding her way barred by the vicar's astonished servants, she threw the summons at them contemptuously and stormed back home. Now she was determined more than ever to continue her campaign against him and the others. The fine she received only infuriated her more.

It has all started the previous year when Phillip Berridge jilted her. Twenty one years of age he was ten years her junior and could not abide her unpleasant attitude towards his friends. To make matters worse, he had become very friendly with Miss Seton Burn, who the vicar employed as a governess. Prudence was determined to win Phillip back at any cost.

By August 1899 she was getting nowhere, whilst Phillip and Seton were talking about becoming engaged. Deciding on drastic measures, Prudence started writing a series of anonymous letters to Phillip, the vicar, Seton and her friend Winnifred Turner. The letters made all manner of scandalous allegations.

Possibly she might have remained undetected, but spite towards the vicar got the better of her. She accused him of committing various crimes and paying Phillip £100 to marry Seton. For some unknown reason she began abusing him verbally at every opportunity. The media of the day chose not to publish her actual words! Within 24 hours of being fined, Prudence was back at her letter writing.

After starting up a campaign to stop the vicar preaching, she transferred her attention to Seton, concentrating on the poor girl's dark complexion. In one letter Seton was called a 'master sweep's daughter'. Also enclosed were some dark bristles cut from a broom. As Winnifred was Seton's friend, she also became a target for Prudence's spite, being accused of unspecified crimes in relation to her nursing the poor. Phillip was accused of being generally immoral.

Realising her hateful letters were getting nowhere, Prudence started another campaign. This time against Phillip whom she wanted run out of Tysoe. It was the last straw and all her victims went to the police. Soon afterwards she was arrested by Sergeant Charles Street.

Prudence continually protested her innocence, even alleging she too had been a victim of the poison pen letter writer. Yet, when challenged she was unable to produce any of the letters. Finally she claimed it was a case of mistaken identity as there were other women in the area called Prudence Hancox.

Sergeant Street was not convinced and found a careful search of her rooms to be most revealing. Among her papers he found an exercise book with loose pages, identical to those on which the letters had been written. On holding her blotting paper to a mirror, he read quite clearly extracts of earlier poison pen letters. When he found a dark broom from which several bristles had been cut, he had enough evidence to charge her with criminal libel.

Meanwhile he employed the services of Thomas Henry Gurrin, a handwriting specialist of many years experience. Thomas came highly recommended by Scotland Yard and the Bank of England. After examining the letters and samples of Prudence's writing, he was adamant. The letters had all been written by one and the same person – Prudence!

In July 1900 she appeared at Warwick Assizes where she pleaded not guilty. She sat impassively whilst the prosecution produced its witnesses. Winnifred could offer no reason for Prudence disliking her so much. Phillip admitted women found him attractive but denied ever having been close friends with the defendant. He had discussed the contents of the first letter with Prudence and wanted to report the matter to the police. However, she had talked him out of the idea.

Finally Prudence entered the witness box to testify on her own behalf. Her defence was simple. She denied having written any letters, explaining how she had lent the exercise book to another girl in the village. When it came back some pages were missing and the blotting paper was in it. When pressed she identified the other girl as a Miss Wilkes who had since left Tysoe. Throughout cross-examination most of her answers were vague, consisting mainly of "I can't remember" and "I don't know."

She explained how the missing bristles had been used by a friend to repair an ornament. When at last she remembered who had used the bristles, the case was adjourned for the woman to be called. When Mabel Pargiter testified, she denied having used the bristles. Then Prudence played her trump card.

She claimed the police had been unable to find her poison pen letters. They were still in her rooms. Following a plea from her lawyer, the judge adjourned the trial again for her to produce them. Under escort Prudence returned to Tysoe the next day. Needless to say, no letters were found.

One of the escorts was Annie Stinchcomb a prison warder who had been instructed to take no part in the search herself, but to watch the prisoner closely. Annie did so and saw her put a pencil and paper into her pocket. Before anybody realised what was happening, Prudence had rushed to the lavatory. Annie was first to reach it. Forcing open the lavatory door, she found Prudence inside just starting to write a poison pen letter to herself. She was taken back to court without any further delay.

Annie testified to what had just occurred in Tysoe. She was followed by Police Constable George Barrett who confirmed he had no knowledge of any other Tysoe residents having received poison pen letters.

Once the jury retired Prudence had to wait about 30 minutes for their verdict. They found her guilty. For the first time she began to show signs of remorse as the judge sentenced her to 12 months imprisonment.

INDEX

94

POLICE

VICTIMS